THE NAKI

(Previously published as "Terror In The Tuli Block")

The "Tuli Block" is a province in the Southern part of Botswana, Africa.

"*Elizabeth.*"

A true story

By Yan Venter

GAL. 2:20
5/13/18

Published by

YVM Books

2426 Crow Mountain Rd

Russellville, AR 72802

USA

First published in the USA in November 2001 by Yan Venter Ministries

Second print in June 12, 2002 by Yan Venter Ministries

Third Print in February 2013, by YVM Books

For information address:

YVM Books, 3426 Crow Mountain Rd, Russellville, AR 72802, USA.

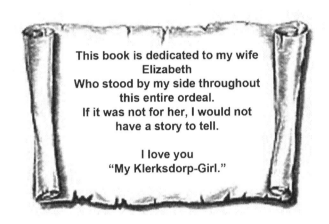

This book is dedicated to my wife
Elizabeth
Who stood by my side throughout
this entire ordeal.
If it was not for her, I would not
have a story to tell.

I love you
"My Klerksdorp-Girl."

ACKNOWLEDGEMENTS

The author has several thanks to extend:

First to my loving family who stood behind me at all times, and who believed in me no matter how big the odds.

To my son, CJ, who proved himself to be a "Jonathan" to me. He proved to be a pillar of strength and a friend through thick and thin.

To my daughter, Reynette, for always believing in me.

You guys are the light of my life.

To my two sisters, Annie and Siennie, together with their husbands, Bertus and Barry, who always lifted me up, and when it was hard to smile at times, they made it possible for me to do so.

To my friend, Rock Hudson, my bookkeeper, for his faithful support, and who would follow me through the most treacherous places.

To my friend, Pastor Larry Pyle, who edited this book under difficult circumstances.

To my brother, Manie Venter, who stood by my side from beginning to end.

To my precious Mother, who have always carried us through every situation with her prayers.

PREFACE

Occasionally in life you meet someone who are a living documentary of the grace of God. Yan Venter is that kind of a man.

When I first met Yan, I recognized that he had a passion for God that would not allow him to deny his destiny. He is a man that has an experience in God, and therefore, he is not at the mercy of men that just live by a set of rules.

Yan's pilgrimage of faith has brought into his life a wealth of freshness, which is contagious. I have laughed with him, as he has laughed at himself. I have wept with him, where he would not have to weep alone and he has done the same for me.

I am glad to say, Yan Venter is my friend, that is the highest recommendation that we can give to anyone. Hi life is like an open book. Now you are privileged to read a few of his pages.

Rev Cleddie Keith

Heritage Fellowship,

Florence, KY, USA.

TABLE OF CONTENTS

INTRODUCTION

After hanging up the phone, I looked at my wife Elizabeth, and said: "Honey, you're not going to believe what has happened. I have to go back to Botswana; Manie needs me!" Although Elizabeth did not say anything, I could see the hurt in her eyes. We were drifting apart. The torrents of life's demands were pulling at us in different directions, and there was nothing I could do about it.

This Ostrich business was placing a demand on our lives, unparalleled to anything that we had faced in our twenty-five years of marriage. The silent strength of this little lady of five feet had helped me through many a tough situation. But, for the first time, we were facing an enemy in our lives greater than anything we had ever encountered before. Separation! Separation, which was not by choice, but by the demand of an international business that asked no questions, but pushed you into a direction that left you no option.

You either moved with the flow, or faced the consequences. Last year, I spent only three months at home, and then the rude persistent ringing of the phone, often interrupted our precious time together.

When she finally decided to say something, it cut through the silence like a knife. "How long are we going to allow this monster to destroy us, Yan?" Her eyes were filled with tears and I knew that if I allowed her the moment, the months of lonely frustration would erupt like a Volcano, and all would be lost. There was just too much tension in the air at that moment. Too much pressure building up inside both of us and I knew that anything said, that wasn't absolutely necessary, would cause harm.

"Honey, I am just as tired. In fact, I am more tired than anyone else in this home. This will be one of the last visits I make to our farm in Botswana. I will be away for only two weeks. This is a promise and I will not break it," I told her. Although I could see that she did not believe me, it still brought her spirit into more calm waters when I said "I am going to hire someone over there that can handle all my responsibilities. That way, I will go to Botswana only once or twice a year."

For several years, I had prayed to God to help me become financially independent so that I could preach as an Itinerant preacher without the burden of hoping that the offerings would cover our expenses. Although God had always supplied our needs, I felt that the need for finances often took me to churches that were not necessarily part of the plan of God. I wanted to be free, to follow the voice of God where He wanted me to go even if I was invited to the small, (often times forgotten) Churches in the country. Churches where faithful Pastors often ministered year in and year out to poor small societies. Churches that often could scarcely afford their Pastor, and when the Evangelist arrived, he would easily walk away with up to three times what that faithful pastor earned week after week.

"God," I said. "I want to be in a position where I can minister to the needs of your people, but also to the needs of your faithful servants."

I knew that I was ready for God to "trust" me in this area. My intentions were pure, and I knew that God had been preparing me for this over the last few years.

I knew something would be coming, but I had no idea it would be this big...

COMMERCIAL EVANGELIST

Ever since we moved to the USA, in 1985, God had demonstrated His faithfulness to our family in supernatural ways.

Wherever I shared our testimony with people, they would always come to me afterwards and say: "Brother Venter, could that be true?"

Over the last eight years, we had been given eight cars. Meetings are scheduled two years in advance and often even during the traditional Christmas weeks, Pastors have pushed their "programs" aside so that Revival meetings could continue.

God has opened doors in places that would be regarded as impossible under normal circumstances. Invitations to preach Camp meetings among all Pentecostal Churches, Southern Baptists, Seventh day Adventists, Catholics, Independents and many more, have rolled in for this Assembly of God preacher.

I knew God was moving me into a road, which I have not traveled on before. It was definitely He. God was performing a remarkable fete in ways uncommon to the human understanding.

The artificial surroundings of the "Commercial Evangelist" had always been repulsive to my spirit. The way they talked about churches, often referring to them as a "giving or non-giving

13

church," reminded me of the way that professional "Bums" were operating in the streets.

When they found a house that appeared sympathetic toward them, they would leave notes for their buddies in certain places, wherein they left addresses and information concerning these good Samaritans.

How easy it is to fall into the same trap. After all, one has to have money to function, to live, to exist.

Must this be the driving force though? Must this be the deciding factor as to where I should go, and how big the churches should be before I accept an invitation to minister?

I have always been a giver myself. I enjoy giving. It is part of my being, and I believe with all my heart that the open hand receives. I am a regular tither, and I believe that my tithes belong to the Church where I receive my spiritual nourishment.

I am convinced in my spirit that there is a lack among many preachers to seek the voice of God first. It is so easy to continue in automatic mode and to end up following your own agenda, instead of doing the will of God.

I do my utmost to retain the call and the thrust of the Holy Spirit. I believe that there is no greater honor bestowed on any human being than to receive the call from God to preach the Gospel of our Lord Jesus Christ.

At every available opportunity I asked God to set me free from the burden of finances. Little did I know that I was literally doing the same as the Israelites in the Old Testament when they asked God for their own king?

God wants us to remain dependent on Him. He wants to take care of us. But this would become the lesson I was to learn in the months to follow.

HEARING THE VOICE OF GOD.

I am convinced that the most precious moments in any Christian's life are the times when he succeeds in hearing the voice of God.

No matter where God sends you or what He tells you to do, you know that it is going to work out because you heard His voice and you *know*, no matter what the cost, God will enable you.

In 1983, while I was a Pastor of a church in South Africa, a certain young man of God paid me a visit. We enjoyed great fellowship, and spoke about the Word for hours. After awhile he asked, *"Brother Venter, what is God saying to you in these days?"*

In a prideful religious manner, I offered him several minutes of religious garbage. After he left, I went down on my knees before God, and cried: "God, I am a successful pastor. Every moment of my life is filled with your work. I spend hours in the Word, and I pray an average amount of time, and yet it's been so long since I've heard your voice!"

I spent hours before the Lord that evening, and I begged for His presence. I begged God to let me hear from Him. I said: "God, here I am, doing your work, teaching your people, building churches, studying your Word, and yet I cannot say that I have heard from you, for so long."

Something was desperately wrong and out of place. If I were to be successful in ministering, (not to my people, but to HIS flock) then I would have to hear from the Holy Spirit.

In society, we are so used to Cliché's of all sorts. For instance we ask: "How are you?" Or "Good morning," and yet we don't really mean it.

In the church, it is exactly the same. They say things like; "Praise God my brother; Glory to His name; Bless God; God bless you," and many more.

In the circles of the Clergy, it is also the same. Many times though, pride will hinder a minister from admitting to this folly because we are supposed to be a step nearer to God.

It sounds so good to be able to say: "Thus saith the Lord," or "I've heard from God." So often though, it is just a cliché, and nothing else.

With the problems we face today, we desperately need men and women who will stand up and say "Thus saith the Lord," and then we can see and know that they have been with the Master.

With diligence I started to listen for His voice in my life. I started paying more attention to listening rather than praying, and it wasn't long before I again started hearing, His voice in my life.

I have never felt at ease with prayerless folk going around with lies or cliché's saying "God told me this or that."

Thank God though, I have met men and women who really walk with Him, and when they say, "God spoke to me, you know they heard His voice."

Their lives bear witness to the fact. The anointing of God is present in their lives, and when you are with them, you are aware that there is something different about them.

God speaks, and when He does, there is the unmistakable assurance that this is God. Then, you don't have to ask yourself: "Is this me? Is it the devil? Or is it really You Lord?"

You just know that it is He. These are glorious moments! How He fills your life with richness. Like an artist, He colors your life with the paintbrush of His magnificence. Your life becomes a storybook, filled with the most dramatic tales.

You become an inspiration to many, and you yearn for the next experience and the next.

Don't misunderstand what I am trying to say to you. I do not mean that my life is without mistakes. It does not mean that I do not step out of line, but what it does mean, is that when I do, I hear Him speak and say: "That is wrong, son. Step this way."

THIS IS NOT FOR YOU . . .

Ministering as Evangelists, Elizabeth and I saw the hand of God active around our lives in the most remarkable ways. We started allowing the Master to control our agenda. It became increasingly easy to only go to places He worked out for us.

There were times when I knew I would go to a certain place even before I was invited. I discovered that I did not have to "shop" around for meetings. I did not have to worry about offerings. We did not have plenty, but we always had enough.

There were times when every available space in our coach, would be packed to capacity with groceries of all kinds. Churches would bless us with generosities and I can truly say: "We had need of nothing."

After preaching a series of meetings in a great Church in Russellville, Arkansas, which lasted for several weeks, I sat in the driver's seat of our Coach, waiting for the engine to warm up. Elizabeth was complaining that we had no more room to put any of the groceries that were given to us. We felt so "blessed", and at the same time, we were making plans to stop this flow of food.

"Honey, we just have to ask the churches from now on, not to give us any more groceries for awhile," I said, and while we were still laughing about this, I felt the presence of the Lord around me. God spoke to my spirit and He said: "You have it all wrong. This blessing is not meant for you, although I let you share in it." I was literally stunned at the clarity of His voice.

I shared this with Elizabeth. We both fell into silence. In fact, we were ashamed at ourselves. We were embarrassed about the way we planned to stop the flow of God and how we were dealing with the blessings of God.

We both started crying. I was sitting there with my head bowed. When I looked up, I saw an old lady across the street. She was digging through garbage cans. God had divinely planned for her to be there at the correct time. Her grocery trolley was filled with garbage. The little lady was a frail, pitiful looking soul, and God said: *"It's meant for her, and others like her."*

I jumped out of the coach, ran across the street and invited the poor lady over for a spree. Hardship was edged all over her face, and for that one moment I wondered if she had any children somewhere, or any family members that cared for her? I could not help but wonder for that one brief moment, what made this creature of God turn into the direction that she was now heading. She was seemingly without hope, without a dream for tomorrow.

Then, as I came back to reality I realized that the reason I was standing in front of her, was not to pry, or intrude. We just needed to bless her. This was the instruction from the Holy Ghost to our spirit.

Suspicion was clearly visible in her eyes as she followed me at a safe distance across the street, where my wife was standing, waiting with a smile

Elizabeth literally opened up the coffers. The baggage bays underneath the Coach were running over with a wealth of food. In fact, we were a grocery store on wheels.

I told the little lady to help herself. She stared at us in astonishment and unbelief. "Help yourself Mom," I said. She took a few cans of food and packed them in her buggy.

"No," I said. "You don't understand. I want you to remove the rubbish from your cart, and fill it up with good stuff. Why push a cart filled with nothing, when you can push it with good things?"

Elizabeth and I had a ball with that little lady. With a little cash in the hand, she was walking away, incessantly looking over her shoulder with a kind of smile that I had not seen in many years, Elizabeth and I sat there with tears running over our cheeks and joy within our hearts. I remembered the words of the Lord when He said: *"It is more blessed to give than to receive."*

As the little lady finally disappeared around the corner with a final wave of the hand, Elizabeth and I looked at each other. Our eyes filled with tears. I could not speak. The lump was too big in my throat. Elizabeth finally broke the joyful silence and said: "Yan, I don't believe I have ever felt the presence and fulfillment of God more in my life than those moments when we helped her get rid of the trash, and fill her cart with those "goodies."

Our joy was complete! In fact, we could actually feel that God was smiling over us. Not because what WE had done, but because HE was able to minister through us.

It was then that God spoke to me again. God spoke things to me, that even though I heard Him say it, I found it difficult to believe. God said: "Once I can see that you can be trusted with what I give, I will give you more."

I quickly said: "God, You can. I know you can! Please make me financially independent. Bring me to a place, where I can bless your Work."

I thought that I was ready. In fact, I just knew I was...

CHAPTER I

THE START OF SOMETHING GOOD

"A WRENCH IN MY HAND."

I believe God puts a person to the test, and as soon as you pass, you are ready to be tested on the next level. There are times when we certainly believe we are ready for "*the big time*," but thank God, He knows better and does not answer our prayers according to "our instructions to Him."

When God finally decided it was time for the next test, this time among the bigger league, I had no idea that I would fail Him so easily. In my thinking I was ready. "I can handle it Lord, try me and see," were the words I would often use in His presence.

It reminds me of my son CJ, when he was just seven years old. I was working on a motorcar engine and was struggling to loosen a nut. Even though I was using an extension to the wrench, the nut just would not move. CJ was standing next to me, watching carefully. Finally, he said: "Dad, give me that wrench. Let me try." I smiled and handed him the wrench.

The little man was serious. The veins swelled up in his neck as he tackled this enormous task. His little knuckles appeared white around the wrench. Groans of agony slipped over his tongue as he attempted to prove to me that he could get the job done. Believe me; the little guy was really trying. He really believed he was capable. Finally, with defeat written all over his face, he handed the wrench back to me and said: "Here Dad, you try again."

In 1992, God finally gave me the wrench that I had been asking for regarding financial independence. I had been telling Him for quite some time that I could handle the job. God handed it to me and then stepped back and watched. Although God knew what was about to follow, I believe He watched with a smile, and waited for the groans of agony and ultimate defeat that would follow.

The Ostrich industry had just opened in the United States, and people were earning great amounts of money.

My brother Manie called from South Africa and told me about this great opportunity. Manie said, "Yan, please make a few calls and find out if we can find any chicks to buy over there."

Manie is my younger brother. I had always enjoyed both my younger brothers. Manie was a definite Entrepreneur. He had the drive in his person that I had always admired. He is always sure of himself, very athletic and certainly an exciting member of our family. Blessed with a great sense of humor, a tender heart towards his fellow man and though not sold out to the Lord yet, he has always revealed a passion for the work of God. I am expecting the Lord to bring him into a close walk with Him.

After many phone calls, I realized that this was indeed a "gold mine" to explore. No one had any chicks to sell. The waiting lists were long and prices for a pair of one-month-old chicks were three thousand dollars! I just could not believe my ears. People were literally falling over each other for these birds.

This marked the beginning of new meat to be introduced into the American meat market. Although the Ostrich meat looked and tasted the same as any prime steak, it was free of any Cholesterol and had less than 3% fat. One pair of Ostriches could produce anywhere from twenty to thirty chicks per season. The skin is very valuable and revived demands for the feathers were reaching into the commercial and Industrial industry. This was becoming an explosive and very attractive investment prospect.

Just as I was about to give up hope in trying to find chicks to purchase, something happened that would bring me to the threshold of a new destiny in my life. A launching pad that would fire me into the outer space of my own fantasy and dream world. I was about to receive the wrench from my Father, which would bring me financial independence. There was no way I could have known this, but this final phone call I was making, would introduce me to the most interesting chapter of my entire life.

The lady I spoke to on the phone also said that they did not have any chicks. But while I was speaking to her, uproar broke out in the background. She excused herself from the conversation for a moment. I waited curiously on the line as I heard people cry in the background. It was obvious to me that a crisis of some sort was hitting the poor people.

Pandemonium broke loose somewhere in their house as I was listening intently with the phone to my ear. I could not make out what was happening, but I realized that something was terribly wrong.

After what seemed like eternity, the kind lady came back to the phone, and told me that her husband just tried to commit suicide. The quiver in her voice revealed the agony she was going through.

Sympathy for the family gripped my heart, and I immediately got into my car and drove the almost 600 miles to their farm in West Texas, to go pay them a visit.

"My name is Yan Venter Ma'am," I said rather clumsily, as she answered the door. "I am the man you spoke with on the phone yesterday about Ostrich chicks, when your husband experienced that enormous problem, and I hope you don't mind that I just showed up here on your doorstep." I explained to the kind lady that I felt a strong desire to pray with the family.

God used me that night. I introduced the man back to the Lord thru prayer. His life was greatly changed, and I made a new friend. He insisted that I sleep over in their home. The following morning the gentleman came and sat on the side of my bed.

"Brother Venter", he said. "I am so impressed with what you did. No one ever showed so much interest in my welfare. Here you are, a stranger, and you drove 600 miles to come and pray for us. I wish I had chicks to sell you, but I don't. I want to do something for you though..."

He continued to tell me about a quarantine station in Los Angeles, that he inherited from someone who owed him a certain amount of money. "I don't know what the quarantine station looks like. I don't even know what is in it. I have never seen it. But I want you to go and check it out. If it is something you can use, it is yours."

I was stunned. I did not expect anything out of this good deed. A quarantine station? What would I do with it? I did not even know what a quarantine station would do! Nevertheless, I decided to go and check it out.

As Elizabeth and I drove up to this quarantine station, we had mixed feelings about it. What would I do with this unusual gift?

As we walked into the place, my amazement knew no bounds. The place was fully equipped to hatch Ostrich eggs! Excitement grew inside of me as I opened one of several brand new hatchers. Everything I needed to hatch Ostrich eggs was there.

Without consulting with God first, I took the leap forward. I just knew this had to be God. It was just too good to be true.

With excitement I dialed Manie's phone number in South Africa. "Manie, I cannot find any chicks to purchase, but if you can find eggs, I have found us a place to hatch them." Laughter broke out, and like a little child with a new toy, I explained to my brother that there were only thirteen Quarantine stations in the nation, and that we were now the proud owners of one of them.

As soon as Manie arrived, work started immediately. We put in many hours of hard work and for the first months we hardly saw our families. With big expenses but not one cent flowing in at first, we had to hang on by our teeth.

However, opportunities that others just dream about came our way. Elizabeth and Hanlie (Manie's wife) saw us maybe once or twice in three months. They were living in the country and we in Los Angeles.

After three months, we earned our first check for $90,000.00. Then within the next three months, a handsome $350,000.00! Within the first year, more than $1,000,000.00 came through our bank account. A year later, Manie and I were millionaires twice over.

When all this started, I told the Lord, I only want to do three batches of eggs, and then I am going to bow out. However something happened that caused me to change my mind, which I will regret for the rest of my life.

As an Evangelist, in times past, God used several people to bless me financially in the ministry. Many of them now heard that I was doing well. I wanted to help them, not realizing that I was once again doing something without asking God about it first.

I already told Manie that he could have the business and that I would step out after the third or fourth batch. Manie understood that my

Ministry was more important to me than the dollars we could make. Now I changed my mind, and told him I would step out only after I helped my friends. Manie was confused, but too gentle to say anything to me to the contrary.

From that point on, everything turned against us. Complete shipments of eggs went missing. Virus after virus hit us in the quarantine station and on the farm in Fresno, CA, where we raised the chicks. The chicks died like flies!

Week after week I wrestled with the thought of my friends losing their investments. I found myself in a spiral, not knowing how to get out of it. I had become a slave to this business. It had me in a death-like grip, and there was no apparent escape. This mad folly became my taskmaster, and I danced according to the tune he was playing. I was trapped and I did not know how to get out of this awful pull.

PUSH THE WHEEL

I felt like Samson, who, at one time defeated the Philistines but now, at the wheel of destiny, I had become the slave of my own desires, with no power to do anything about it. I was left with no escape. My friends' investments were at stake, and there was absolutely no escape from this mad venture.

With very few Ostrich egg suppliers in South Africa; the competition on the market soon became fierce. Egg prices skyrocketed from $100.00 to $350.00 an egg within one year. The prices were without any fertility guarantees and the farmers sold us just about anything they could lay their hands on.

These money-crazed farmers in Namibia, at times, even sold us rotten eggs.

I recall once purchasing 1600 eggs and only 11% of the batch was fertile! That meant we paid $336,000.00 for 1344 eggs that were totally useless!

We knew we just had to get our own farm in Africa as soon as possible. The whip of a relentless taskmaster was on my back, and all that was expected of me was to keep on pushing this wheel of madness.

Several times in the early stages of the business venture, God created windows of opportunity for me to pull out, but my stubborn nature thought that one more batch was needed.

Looking back today I can hardly believe how blind I became with this lust for fortune and fame.

I cannot believe how easily I actually failed the test, and how I allowed self to stand in the way of what I knew to be right.

Life is full of lessons though, and as long as you don't pass the same way twice, your life becomes enriched by yesterday's mountains and rivers we have to cross.

Another one of the problems for the importers was the air transportation. Everything depended on rapid delivery. The eggs were to be in the incubator no later than fourteen days from the day they were laid. It was also of utmost importance that the eggs arrived with minimum air sac disturbance.

One of my good friends invested with us and we purchased a load of eggs for him. As we stood at the Airport, waiting for the eggs to be offloaded, our surprise knew no bounds as we discovered that the entire shipment was not on board.

No one seemingly knew what had happened to the eggs. Frantic efforts from both sides of the two continents achieved nothing and for more than ten days the Airline Company tried to locate the missing shipment.

One must understand, it is not like your luggage that ends on the wrong flight. A batch of eggs like that, are big enough to fill a regular size living room from top to bottom. A good size Ostrich egg weighs an average of two and a half pounds each.

The shipment was finally tracked down in France, and when the eggs arrived at their destination in Los Angeles, they were in the worst of condition.

Manie and I stood horrified as they off-loaded our precious cargo from the Aircraft.

Some of the boxes were stepped on and others were wet. Some of the eggs were now twenty-two days old and most of them did not even have an air sac anymore.

It was one big disaster. We could not believe our eyes. Over $400,000.00 in scrambled eggs!

Once again, the whip was on my back and all I could do was push and push...

I soon realized that I had a wrench in my hand and I was working on a nut that was far more stubborn than I had ever imagined and my heavenly Father was standing back, watching me wrestle with this very tough situation.

Believe me, I wanted to hand it back to the Lord. The only thing is, I did not know where He had gone. I left Him somewhere behind in the marsh of selfish ambition and mistaken decisions...

CHAPTER 2

THE BEGINNING OF TERROR

"BACK TO AFRICA."

As I stepped off the Airplane in Windhoek, Namibia, the desert air was thick. Turtledoves were lazily sitting around in Kameeldoring (Camel thorn trees) trees around the parking lot, and it seemed as if the heat was even too much for them.

Namibia had set an example for the Republic of South Africa on the Political arena. Apartheid was removed and the remarkable success they experienced between races caused the people in South Africa to push toward the same goal. This small Country was doing well economically and the air was filled with excitement. Everyone seemed so happy and peaceful.

The spirit of Democracy opened many doors, and especially for us in the USA, it was good for the Ostrich business. Namibia removed almost all restrictions from the import/export business and thus opened the door wide for worldwide participation in this rapid expansion of the Ostrich Industry. Manie and I realized by now, if we did not do something about the egg situation, we would not be able to survive this race. With egg prices rising very rapidly, and farmers selling us any scrap they had on hand, something had to be done.

I was sent back to Africa to investigate the possibilities of purchasing our own farm and stocking it with Ostriches.

Namibia was first on our list of priorities. They had a large number of Ostriches, and it seemed as if there would be no problem with getting the eggs exported from there.

The vast open beauty of Namibia with its desert on the one hand and the Ocean, with miles of white beaches on the other hand, is enough to impress any person who has a love for nature.

At first glance, it almost appears as if nothing can live in this desolate area, but at closer range, a world of its own is revealed. A variety of wild life strikes you suddenly as you open your eyes to what lies behind the seemingly hot open horizons.

It is not only the rich diamond deposits in the soil of Namibia that makes this country so wealthy, but also in spite of obvious water shortage, farmers are thriving.

Now, to add to this good fortune, many of these farmers find themselves blessed beyond comprehension since the Ostrich market exploded in the United States.

After traveling on a lonely and narrow road for days into the heart of this beautiful country, an angry baboon barked with alarm as if to tell me to get away from here.

I smiled at him and told myself, that he reminded me of the farmers I had met over the last two days.

I had discovered that these Namibian farmers frowned at the idea of an American coming into their profitable circle. They closed ranks and all of a sudden no one had any Ostriches for sale. The ones that were still offered to me were inferior and ridiculously over priced.

As I parked the little rental car at the front of the house, I had a strange feeling that this visit, like all the previous ones, would end in the same disappointment.

The way this prospective Seller greeted me, I had a suspicion that he was alerted to my presence and with an obvious lack of hospitality, that was so common to these areas, I was received outside and it took only a few minutes to find out that I was not going to get anywhere with him either.

It is truly amazing how easy it is to take that wrench in one's own hand, and wrestle with something that you know is too big for you. Instead of giving it straight back to "Father" who is more than capable of handling these situations, you carry on and on.

Looking back at your own past, and drawing the curtain of memory back so that the stage of your own play in life is once again revealed, you often sit there as part of the audience and marvel at your own stubbornness.

If ever there is something I've learned to appreciate about our Lord, it is the patience and long-suffering, He exhibits towards His children. All of these personal endeavors and activities are part of a lesson. They are not un-forgiven, but they are lessons to be learned. Sometimes *very* expensive ones, but at the end they serve to enrich your life even more.

"Namibia is now scratched off the agenda," I mumbled after I strapped myself safely into the seat of the Boeing 737, which would take me back to Johannesburg, South Africa.

I only realized that I was talking out aloud after an old gentleman sitting next to me, looked over to my side and smiled as if to indicate that he understood why men started talking to themselves after a certain age.

I nodded my head reluctantly in his direction, but then closed my eyes as an indicator that I had no desire to develop a discussion.

Next, we looked at the country of Swaziland, and again I pursued avenue after avenue.

My youngest brother, Dries, joined me in this dreary task of trying to find suitable land.

Dries, the youngest in our family, had the same fighting spirit in him as Manie and I.

Upon my return from Namibia, he came and stood in front of me, and smilingly said, "You've been out of Africa far too long brother. Let me show you how things are done here now-a-days."

The question in my eyes, prompted him to continue. "I will accompany you to Swaziland, Yan. Take with you enough cash to look good."

He laughed out loud, but I noticed nevertheless that he was serious.

Sitting now in the plush Restaurant in Swaziland with the Minister of Agriculture as our guest, I could not believe how easily Dries had managed to achieve this difficult task.

Each time he paid the waiter he deliberately flashed a thick roll of American dollars and I could not help but notice the greedy expression on the face of this important man.

This time, doors were swinging open wide for us. Influential men in top Governmental Cabinet positions went out of their way to assist us.

We were treated like royalty. Mr. Themba, the Minister of Agriculture, personally took us around, and at times when he was not available, he would graciously offer his second in command who would spend hours with us trying to find suitable land for our venture.

No stone was left unturned. We were offered a variety of the most beautiful land and we could choose at our leisure.

After a very expensive meal, the Minister took the white Napkin to his face. His eyes were sparkling with excitement. His lovely wife was sitting quietly next to him, and I could not help but to feel like a mouse in the claws of a cat, when he looked over to me.

"Well, Mr. Venter, it seems as if you have finally found suitable land?" We laughed, his belly shaking up and down. I noticed the quick glance between his wife and him. They were happy, but so were we.

The music around us carried the loud beat of Africa. The air was hot and humid. A fan above us was turning lazily and I noticed the dust on its blades. I reminded myself that this was the way things are done in Africa. If it is not absolutely necessary to clean, if it is not too visible, then it will be left alone until needed.

I also noticed that a few fly stickers were hanging from the ceiling with a load of flies stuck to it.

At the end of the meal, the minister lifted his glass of expensive wine ceremoniously. "To our partnership!" Once again, his belly flopped up and down during his outrageous spell of laughter.

Dries, glanced over to me while he joined the merriness. "To the partnership," we both cried out in unison while we lifted our glasses of coke.

I was excited beyond words, but a strange feeling of nagging concern was hanging over my head and it was restricting my spontaneity. I could not explain it, but it was definitely there.

"Tomorrow, you come to my office and all the permits you need will be waiting for you. " He said this underneath another outbreak of loud laughter. His belly shook some more and his quite little wife only laughed when he looked in her direction.

Was I just imagining this, or was this hard nut giving in at last?

Across the table from us, two sinister looking men were staring at us and when I greeted them, their demeanor was one of aggression. It was obvious that they had been listening to our conversation.

A strange feeling of unrest now gripped my spirit. I knew that we were doing everything legal, but something was not right.

Months later the same two men would again appear on the scene, this time ready to throw me in jail...

SO CLOSE AND YET SO FAR

"Mr. Themba, how can this be?" I looked with unbelief at the Minister of Agriculture after he had just informed me, that no permits would be forthcoming.

His ashamed face told me that this was no joke. The festive spirit of last night was no longer there, and he appeared so lonely behind his expensive desk in this large office.

His soft belly appeared more bloated than last night, but the only difference was that it was not bouncing up and down with laughter. The man was serious.

"You promised me from the beginning that permits would not be a problem! In fact, last night around the dinner table, you told me that I would pick them all up today?"

How could something so good, go wrong, so fast? My head was spinning. When I spoke to Elizabeth the previous evening, I told her about our success, and everyone at home was happy. I was coming home with an Ostrich Farm in my pocket.

My protest was really weak. I realized that something drastic must have gone wrong. Mr. Themba was offered to become a silent partner in the business with a percentage of our profits. This amounted to a substantial amount of money for him.

"Is it money that you want, Mr. Themba? Are we not offering you enough?" The man was sitting behind his desk. His shoulders were drooping, and there was an expression of genuine regret and defeat in his voice when he answered me.

"Yan, I have grown to like you very much. You are the type of person I would put my life in your hands. I have been looking forward to building on this relationship, but something happened this morning that is beyond my control."

I was sitting there, fixed to my chair. It was almost as if the world around me was collapsing. I felt sick. The tension inside me was great, and at the same time, I felt so defenseless.

After so many months and so many miles, I found myself at a point where I suddenly realized that this is once again a dead end street.

Swaziland had suddenly become just another dream that had also gone up in smoke. I was looking at this sad man, but I did not see him. I saw the smoking remains of a dream. Only the ashes, and it all happened so suddenly.

Painfully slow, the man looked up at me, and for a moment I almost thought that there was a tear in his eye. His voice was emotional when he explained to Dries and I, that the South African Government had been in contact with him that morning, and threatened to close trade relations with Swaziland should he continue with this venture.

"Mr. Themba, how did they even know about me, or about our intended venture? Can the South African Government really tell you how to run your country?

Are you not allowed to conduct business as you wish?

Are you not a Sovereign State and recognized as such by the United Nations?" The questions rolled over my tongue like a paper shredder spitting out shreds of paper remains.

The Minister shook his head in agreement while I was rattling down one question after another. At the end he slowly explained to me with his hands folded around his round belly, that although this was so, his country is land-locked and therefore totally dependent on the infrastructure of South Africa. He explained that without the assistance of that country no imports and exports could take place and that he could not afford to jeopardize the relationship.

Suddenly I ran out of questions. A lame feeling gripped my being, and the excitement of this morning gave way to a feeling of depression. For several minutes no one had anything to say. The Minister avoided my glance like a little boy who had just lost his marbles in a match with a bully.

Finally I walked out of his office with disgust and anger in my spirit. I came so close, only to see all my efforts slip through my fingers like water and disappearing into dry ground.

Dries was very quite next to me. We were both shocked.

Outside, the same two sinister looking men from the Restaurant the previous night were leaning against a lamppost looking at us with a grin on their faces.

For several minutes I just sat in my car, not ready to move. I did not move because I was not sure where I should go now. I was a man without destiny.

I am a fighter, and I don't take "No" for an answer easily, but what was I to do now? The only obvious thing was to go home.

Suddenly that thought appealed to me, and as I drove off, I took one last look at Mr. Themba's office. For a moment, I thought I saw him standing there, but then the glare of the morning sun disturbed my vision.

What I was not mistaking about however was the car that pulled out of the parking lot behind me. It was the same two men. I decided to ignore them for now.

In front of me was a sign which read: "JOHANNESBURG", and without any second thought about the men behind me, I headed for that city where I would board that beautiful Leviathan of the skies that would take me home.

Home is where I wanted to be now more than ever before.

I still had the wrench in my hand though and although I was tired, I was not yet ready to hand it to my Father. The real lesson would still come, and it would hurt more than anything I had ever experienced in my life

"TRY IT THIS TIME."

"Honey, the phone is ringing!" My wife's voice, and a gentle poke in the side, caused me to sit up in bed. Totally confused by my surrounding. I could not see what time it was in the dark.

I scrambled out of bed and ran into a wall, totally disoriented. I had only been home from Swaziland for a week.

"Hey Yan, are you still sleeping?" It was 2am in the morning. The voice on the other side sounded like he had just won a Jackpot, and wanted to crow to someone else about it. With a sleepy voice, resembling an old croaky toad, I mumbled a "hello", still wandering if this was some kind of emergency.

"Speak up man, I can't hear you," the voice said on the other side.

I was irritated at the man's distant rebuke so early in the morning, but about that time I realized I had the phone upside down next to my face.

"Yan, this is Mike. Can you hear me now?" Mike is a friendly Greek businessman in South Africa. We had been buying eggs from him on several occasions and he knew that we were looking to buy an Ostrich farm.

In fact, I had come to find out that he knew everything that was going on in the business. Mike made it his business to know.

When you mention the name "Mike Englesaki" someone is about to either hate the man or speak highly of him.

He had treated us fairly, and I had no reason to be suspicious.

"I have a great proposition to make to you." I could not believe my ears. Mike did not make propositions. He had always been in the driver's seat.

"I have an Ostrich business for sale in Botswana. There are about twelve hundred Ostriches, and they are all exportable immediately. You can be rolling within the next season."

Suddenly I was wide-awake.

"Wow Lord," I said to myself. "I had just been defeated in Africa and now this? I had been chasing all over the African Continent, trying to find something like this and now it just fell into my lap at 2:00am!

Mike explained to me that he was in partnership with two other people and he needed to get out of that situation as soon as possible.

"The man who owned the farm, where these birds are, is just not honest and I want to break ties with him as soon as possible," he continued to explain.

I excused myself, ran to the bathroom where I knew he could not hear me, and gave one big shout. Calmly, I returned to the phone.

Elizabeth sat up straight with a curious expression. "What's going on?" she asked in a whisper, knowing that I was onto something good. I signaled to her to wait and then put the phone back to my ear.

With a slight tremor noticeable in my voice, I tried to sound as normal as possible. "We'll take it Mike, What do you need from us?"

In a smiling tone, Mike said, " I knew you would. Send me a deposit of sixty thousand today, and get here as soon as possible."

We discussed a few more details and then I hung up the phone.

Without trying to hear the voice of God, or to find out what God had to say about this matter, I turned to my wife and told her about the *"wonderful"* opportunity which had just opened up for us.

I reached for the telephone again, and called my brother Manie.

"Manie, are you still sleeping?" We both laughed in a silly way about this unnecessary question.

"What's going on?" Manie wanted to know, and for the next several minutes I informed him about this turn of events.

"Well, we need to get there as soon as possible, don't you think? Before someone else gets in ahead of us."

I was so sure that this was a door opening for us that I did not even bother about looking up to the Father to see if He would agree.

Sleep was no longer an option and as Elizabeth made us a welcome cup of coffee, I started singing in the shower. I sang the song of Africa.

I sang about the mountains, the baboons, and the hungry lion stalking its prey. It was a silly song, but I wanted to give vent to my exuberant emotions.

I felt so sure that this was the best thing that could happen to us.

"How long are you going to be away this time?" Elizabeth asked her question with a quiver in her voice and a cup of coffee in her hand.

"Honey, I have no idea, but you will understand, that we must grab this opportunity with both hands.

Because I noticed the last remains of a questioning frown in her face, I continued to drive the nail a little deeper by saying: "I have to do this. God has opened this door for us…"

She had always trusted my decision-making, but was I mistaken, or was she displaying a turn your nose up at me instead of a smile. I ignored this signal and months later I wished I had not.

YES SIR, MR. PRESIDENT.

After traveling so many miles, spending so much money and being away from my family for so long, I could not believe that we had finally arrived at the place where our plans would now come together.

Seated now in the luxury of the Botswana's State President's office, I waited for *THE MAN* to come out and see me.

A few hours ago I was told that *The President* himself wanted to see me immediately. I wasn't sure exactly what to expect. Upon my arrival I was treated like royalty.

Guards came to attention and loudly clicked their heals together and saluted me as a Civilian when I arrived at the gate. When I introduced myself to these soldiers, they immediately stood aside and told me with a smile to pass thru as "El Presidente" was expecting me."

As I walked up to the large front of the Presidential Palace his Excellency's personal secretary was waiting to welcome me. His smile made me feel uncomfortable and the President's security guards carried out the routine duty by running their hands clumsily over my person to search for any concealed weapons.

He was a thin, funny, strange looking man, with thick, dark glasses. He was neatly dressed in a dark suit, but I immediately noticed that his shirt collar was dirty and felt tempted to adjust his tie, which needed adjustment.

The teacup in my hand was embossed with gold, and I could hardly believe that I was actually sitting as a personal guest in the sitting room of the state president of Botswana. This man was regarded as one of the top leaders in Africa.

The air was hot and sticky and a lonely fly was constantly trying to get into my cup of tea. All of this however, was only slightly observed as my mind raced back to the events of the last few days since I arrived in Botswana.

We purchased the entire Ostrich inventory, which consisted of almost 900 breeding females. Several days later, we signed a lease for land, which was ideally situated for the Ostrich farm.

The farm was nestled in between two large mountainous sections and very private.

The roads to the farm were terrible and I was wondering how we were going to get the eggs from the farm to the nearest airport.

The enormous task of transporting these very temperamental birds to the farm was lying ahead.

Our newly acquired farm needed to be developed. Fences had to be put up. Roads needed to be constructed and water to each camp needed to be installed.

"God, I don't know when I will see my family again," I sighed and whispered to myself.

All these questions and many more were flashing through my mind continuously, but I assured myself that this too would pass.

I was at the licensing office of the Department of Wildlife, trying to find out about all the requirements and rules and regulations for the intended exports, when the official informed me of the President's desire to see me.

I could not believe my ears. "You mean the State President of Botswana wants to see me before I get my license?" The Wildlife official smiled and assured me, that I was very special. He explained to me that this was a rare privilege. Somehow I did not believe the man, and when I left the office, a weird feeling took a hold of me.

The stubborn fly had now obviously changed his mind (I don't know if flies have a mind) and was now trying its best to get up my nose instead of my teacup. As I slapped my own face, a door leading somewhere into an adjoining room opened up and the President appeared with the smile of a used-car salesperson.

Behind him, was his funny looking secretary, with the perpetual smile stuck to his face and I could not help but notice that his tie still needed adjustment. I also noticed that his eyes were not smiling. He was holding a writing pad in his hand and he appeared like a man, standing in the shadow of a huge, tree.

The President was neatly dressed. I guessed his age to be in the middle sixties. I noticed that he was carrying his age very well. He possessed an electrifying personality and spoke to me in perfect English.

"A-ha, the man from America, or is it more accurate to say that Mr. Ostrich himself is honoring me with his presence," he said with a rare enthusiasm for such an important man.

"I heard about your business venture here in our country, Mr. Venter," and he seated himself right close to me, on the same couch.

He was the personification of a Politician. "He had an agenda, that is for sure." I told myself, as I smiled back at him.

I tried not to show my suspicion and for the next few minutes, I shared in his jovial, but uninteresting conversation.

The room was sticky, and the fly was not interested in the president. The thing was buzzing around my head as if he was acting under a remote control.

The president smiled as I missed in an attempt to catch the fly, but said nothing.

Finally I said: "Well Mr. President, you asked to see me, and I am honored to be here, but I am so curious to find out what this invitation is all about?"

With a political smile fixed to his face, he sat a few inches closer to me.

Just as he was about to speak, he acted as if he remembered something, and then paused for a moment.

He looked over his shoulder to his personal Secretary, and with a slight nod of the head in the direction of this wimpy little man, he disappeared from the room.

As the little man shuffled out of the room, he reminded me of a little puppy dog, obeying the command of his master.

I grew up in Africa, and I know that some of these leaders are power crazy. They are dangerous men, who can make you disappear anytime they want to. Some of them also have no problem doing so. Although this man was no Idi Amin, and the leader of a democratic country, I was still not feeling at ease.

I assured myself that I was an American citizen, and therefore under her protection.

The President waited until the door clicked shut behind the secretary before he started to speak again.

"Word reached me about the Ostrich industry in America and also your company's investment here in my Country."

I nodded my head in agreement, but waited for him to continue.

"I want to get involved in this game also."

He paused after this opening statement and searched my eyes for any response. For a while, I couldn't help but to feel like a mouse in front of a hungry cat. I knew I had to move real carefully.

For the next few minutes, he told me that he was reaching the end of his first term, but that he was positive, he would be allowed to serve one more term.

"At the end of my final term as President, I would have to find something to do," he said. "And this is where you come in."

He laughed when said it, but I picked up a warning sign in his voice.

The President made me understand that we would have no real problems with our exports, as long as he could also get involved.

Very carefully I explained to him that I was only one partner in this corporation, and that the others would have to be approached on this matter.

"Good," he said, as he stood up from the Coach. "I am sure that you will explain to them very well."

When I was ready to leave the office of the president, it was with a sense of relief, but also with a sick feeling of suspicion inside me that this could be the beginning of real trouble for us.

I gave the ugly, blue fly one more angry look while it was sitting on the brim of my teacup, and walked out of the office.

THIS TOO WILL BE DONE.

I was the first to wake up on the farm. Everyone finally joined us the previous evening. My two sisters, Sienie and Annie, with their two husbands joined our work force. Dries was there, and Manie was as excited as myself to get this huge project off the ground. Fourteen Kilometers of fencing had to be put up. Eight kilometers of roads had to be constructed. Trees had to be removed, trenches had to be dug for the kilometers of water pipe to be installed.

We realized that we did not have much time to get all this work done, as the newly acquired ostriches had to be removed from the other farm. Mike Englesaki's partner on the farm was as mean as a junkyard dog and we did not trust him.

The previous night was spent in a festive mood. The great barbeque fires were lit and the exciting Afrikaner Boer[1] Music filled the night skies. We laughed, some danced and everything was as it should be in Africa. Relaxed and yet ever ready, because in this country you never know what may jump at you around the next bend.

Late that night after the entire crew retired to their rooms, I hung around for a while longer to give my mind a chance to reflect on the events of

---

[1] "Boer" is a nickname that was given to the early South African Pioneers.

the recent days. I was not tired, but I certainly felt weariness and the thought of this wrench in my hand was with me.

The silhouette of an aged Baobab tree in the reflection of the fires, gave an almost creepy atmosphere to the events around the house. Finally, after sitting around for another hour listening to the night sounds around me, I also made my way to bed.

Since early this morning, I was listening to the call of the Jackal. The first cry sounded from afar, but then close to the house, the answer of the second one was heard later. The night air was humid; the fans in the room just could not do the job of keeping the heat under control. The windows could not be opened for fear of the barrage of mosquitoes. I decided that one of our first tasks would be to get mosquito nets in front of the windows. This heat was just unbearable.

Finally, the leader of a troop of baboons barked out the news that the new day was here. The persistent sound of his annoying bark caused me to get up and walk outside. The sun was barely managing to get its first hold on the day, and already the effects of it could be felt. Over in the distance I noticed a Kiewiet bird circling its nest on the ground and with its high pitch whistle, it almost sounded if it protested the noise of the old baboon leader up on the hill outside of the farmhouse.

Ten minutes later I had a fresh pot of coffee brewing on the stove. The house was filled with the aroma of coffee beans boiling.

Lights came on all around in the house, and in one of the rooms, Barry, Sienie's husband turned on the news. One of the most important things in South Africa is the news. So much is happening daily. Mandela was reaching the daily headline news, and this morning was no exception. Mandela was addressing an angry mob of Xhosa warriors, who marched with tens of thousands wearing the traditional warrior outfits. The atmosphere in South Africa was explosive! Mr. Buthelezi, the Zulu Chief was mustering his warriors and the country was literally buzzing with the idea of a civil war about to break out. The elections were soon to take place, and for the first time in the history of the country every one would get a chance to vote.

It was noticeable that everyone in the house had their ears tuned to the news on the radio, and Barry also knew to turn it up loud enough for all to hear.

Bertus, our Manager on the farm, is a silent, yet very strong character. No work is ever too much for him to handle. This morning as he appeared in the kitchen, dressed in khaki shorts and shirt, with his pipe clenched between his teeth, he was a picture of a typical South African Boer. His muscular body and easy stride cautions you that he is not the type of person you would want to have as an enemy.

Barry, Bertus' older brother had always been my friend. Like Bertus, he is not the normal talking type, but one you can always depend on. He and Sienie had been so close to me through the years. As they now walked into the kitchen, Sienie walked around the table and lovingly put her arms around my neck. "My boetie[2] she

---

[2] Pronounced: "Bootie" – meaning little brother.

said, "I am so happy to be with you and Manie on this historic day. Thank you for allowing Barry and me to be part of this venture.

Sienie and Annie are both so giving in nature. They are both loving and easy to get around with. "Manie and I are so fortunate to have these two couples as staff members on our farm," I thought to myself.

Our day was started, like all other days, with Bible reading, prayer and a few songs before we would take the last sip of coffee and head out the door.

Our workers were standing ready outside. The trucks and earth moving machines were all ready the day before. We divided into three teams, just as we arranged the previous night. Each team taking care of a different task, and by lunchtime, even I was amazed at how much we achieved in such short time.

Drilling the thousands of holes for the fence poles was no easy task. Manie was at the head of this team and he was making good time. All he had on was his small boxer shorts and a cap. His already dark complexion quickly reacted to the hot Botswana sun, and soon he was as black as an ace of spades.

Suddenly, my ears picked up the noise of the high revving tractor engine, which Manie was operating. I was just in time to see the tractor flip over backwards. Manie's boxer shorts got hung up somewhere on the seat beside him, but there was no time to grab for them. He rolled off to the side of the tractor with his boxer shorts still hung up around his ankles, revealing the handsome suntan around the rest of his body. The air broke out with laughter all around Manie, but minutes later he was back at work again.

News reached farmers near and far about how fast the infrastructure of the farm went up, and some of them even took time to come and see for themselves. Our neighbors were there at the end of each day, to come and see the progress. They could not believe their eyes. These were seasoned farmers who were involved in this kind of work all their lives.

Even the women were involved in a beehive of activity, and Annie turned the old looking house into an attractive home.

Nine days later, we started up the trucks to go and fetch the precious cargo of birds.

Nearly twelve hundred Ostriches had to be moved over horrible conditions on the Botswana roads.

We were ready. Everything was in place, and once again, like a smooth grinding machine, everyone knew his or her place. As the Ostriches arrived on the farm, they were treated with a variety of precautionary medicines, numbered and carefully released into their individual camps. Annie and Sienie labored in the extreme Botswana sun, with straw hats as big as Sombreros offering a little relief. Every now and then, they would spray themselves and everyone else around them with a water hose. For brief moments, laughter would break out, but then the same backbreaking work would recommence.

At one time the wild nature in Annie took over and she jumped on the back of one of the ostriches. The ride was a wild one, with the ostrich spinning around and around but Annie clung to its wings for dear life until the ostrich finally came to a halt. Once again the air was filled with laughter.

At last, the final long day ended when all the birds were transported, and each camp was filled with its allocated amount of birds. Although we were all tired and worn out, no one would think about going to bed, without thanking God in a sweet, memorable, moment of prayer. We did not lose one bird! It was an achievement that even Mike Englesaki said, could not be done.

Only one bird seriously injured his sensitive neck. Dries stepped in front of me when I suggested to have the bird put down. He felt sure that he would save the life of this precious animal. With the help of a half-inch water pipe and many bandages, he constructed a neck brace. It was a sight to see this animal running around with this straight neck, but "old straight neck," as we nicknamed him, would survive and offer his part of egg production in the ensuing months.

All we needed now was for these birds to lay eggs. That was going to take time, but we were ready. The birds were moved three months before the egg-laying season would commence. We were ready for the job, or so we thought...

The activities in the yard were peaceful, with everyone involved in their tasks. Annie's dog was engaged in a wrestling match with another, while she was putting a vegetable garden together, when suddenly, the silence over the farm was broken.

Two helicopters appeared over the ridge with no regard for the safety of the highly sensitive Ostriches. Pandemonium broke out. Manie came running out of the barn with arms swinging, fists waving at the unconcerned pilots, but they kept on circling the pens. Ostrich birds ran wildly into the fences, some injuring themselves. Annie's grandchild started screaming hysterically and some of the local people who had never seen this kind of activity, stood mesmerized in one position.

Army vehicles rolled into the yard and we were told to expect the State President. The normally quiet Bertus was beside himself, and in his broken English let them have a piece of his mind: "You stupid, bloody people. What you try to do? You trying to killing our birds?" The commander radioed for the helicopters to move away, and the situation came back under control.

We were told that the President would visit our farm later that day, and that if we wanted, we could prepare dinner for him.

The army personnel proceeded to set up the perimeter. It looked as if war was about to break out.

A few hours later the man himself arrived on our farm with about forty additional guards. He expressed interest in our welfare like a Python would look at his victim before the strike. Manie was asked to carefully explain how everything works. Our workers who were all Botswana

60

citizens would not go to work until they all came and personally greeted their President. Just a week before, Sienie and Annie handed each of them a couple of sets of overalls. All of them now appeared in the same color uniforms, and proudly came and shook the President's hand.

"So, Mr. Venter, I understand that you are one of the other partners in this good business?" His snake eyes searched Manie for any sign of weakness, after which, he would make his strike. Manie was not displaying any such sign of weakness at all. The recent events with the circling helicopters were still too fresh in his mind. Irritation was still in most of their minds for the reckless way in which this Monte crew approached our property. Our birds were nervously running into the fences, injuring themselves. Bertus had his hands full to bring the situation back under control.

"Yes sir, Mr. President, that's me" and without stopping, proceeded to refer to my previous visit with him in his office, and his interest in our business.

The conversation was interrupted when food fit for a king was carried outside on long tables. Sienie and Annie were putting their best foot forward. A variety of meats and food were set on the table. The President reached forward to dish up, but then Sienie suddenly spoke up and said: "Shall we first say grace Mr. President?" An awkward smile appeared on his face, and then Barry prayed.

"Well Mr. Venter, so what did the other partners have to say about my interest in your business? He asked, as soon as he was handed his cup of coffee at the end of the meal.

"Mr. President, the other partners in the United States have decided not to take in any additional partners at this time, but to offer you all the assistance you may need to put together your own place."

The atmosphere became real cold, and everyone around the table noticed the look on his face. He did not like the idea of being said "NO" to. Sienie noticed his sudden glance over to his personal secretary who was never without his writing pad.

Manie and Bertus took him around the farm and explained every detail to him. They explained to him exactly why the USDA wants the double fencing around the entire perimeter. The atmosphere was thick and although the man was trying to remain friendly, it was now more an official visit than before the meal started.

"I don't see why I must have this width between the double fence. It will take too much effort to keep it clean." As he spoke this way, anyone could see, that the man was used to getting his way. "Mr. President, you must understand the USDA is not going to approve you unless you do as they require." He threw his arm up in the air and spoke like a typical Las Vegas gambler. "I have diplomatic ties Manie, that will make it a little more easy." He laughed, and the sound of his laughter echoed through the valley below. Behind him, his personal secretary and the rest of his crew giggled about his statement, and all of them nodded their heads, as if to say, "He can do anything, he wants to."

An Uneasy feeling filled the air and surrounded the group. "Yes Mr. President." Manie knew that the USDA would not approve the man's farm for export to the United States unless it would meet with their standard. Turning the President down would spell immediate trouble for all of us.

When I came back from Johannesburg the following day, after a brief visit, I learned of the President's visit to our farm. Around the kitchen table, everyone wanted to get his or her word in. Bertus was still puffing angrily on his pipe. Sienie was laughing about the way she taught the man how to pray, and Annie laughed and told me how she almost spilled coffee on his lap. Everyone laughed about the way Barry said his prayer in Afrikaans, and Manie told me how the president's security guards almost arrested Bertus when he reached for his pipe in his pocket. They thought that he had a concealed weapon.

Bertus added to the happy atmosphere by saying in his normal dry manner, "I was so mad at them for scaring our birds the way they did, that I was going to blow him over with my smoke."

"What I want to know, is what was his response when you told him that we were not opening the business for him to join Manie?" I held my breath, because I know Africa, and so did everyone else.

"Oh, my boetie," Sienie jumped in first. "You should have seen the way he looked over his shoulder at his Secretary. I don't trust the man at all." Everyone agreed.

"He is not going to cooperate with the USDA with regards the double fencing. He is stubborn and that is going to cause trouble for us," Bertus, said. We were in deep trouble, and I did not know how to get out of it.

Our suspicions and fears came true a few weeks later, when our farm was approved for export and "EL PRESIDENTO" was turned down on his farm.

Up until today, we never saw or heard from the man again, but that day the horizons of our lives were filled with dark, stormy clouds.

Weeks later, as I came out of the office of the Department of Wildlife, I was startled when I noticed the two familiar faces of my followers from before. They did not even try to hide themselves. They were looking at me with condescension.

I looked around, with the wrench in my hand, and I was trying to hand it back to my father in heaven, but He was nowhere to be found. I had walked away from Him, months ago, and I was on my own. I knew it all too well.

EGGS IN THE BASKET

Sienie is my older sister and she practically raised me as a kid. She was indeed a loyal friend and she and Barry were such incredibly hard workers, like every one else on the farm. I knew I could always depend upon them.

Annie, one of my younger sisters, is always very sensitive towards other people's needs and like Sienie, a very hard and faithful worker. She and Bertus, her husband, were managing the farm for us.

As I drove up to the gate of the farm, I was still confused about the absence of God in my spirit. I was tired and homesick for my family whom I now had not seen for three months. The first export permit was neatly folded in my briefcase.

"Father, when I get back home, I'm stepping out of this thing. I don't care if I lose everything. I just want to be back where I belong."

For the first time in my walk with God, I felt like a "Prodigal." I knew I could go home, but I kept believing that tomorrow everything would clear up and I would return with "honors."

I found a real festive spirit on the farm. Everyone knew I was coming with the export permit. Music was playing loud and everyone was happy. Some of the black people were dancing happily under the shade of a big old sycamore tree. Fires were lit and tables were neatly set for a party to begin outside. Meat was brought to the fire in typical African style. In the late afternoon the scorching sun was at last prepared to let off on the relentless heat wave and turtledoves were loudly joining in with the festive spirit. Even the Baboons outside on the little hill, next to our farm, seemed a little more rowdy than normal. As I looked towards them, it seemed as if the entire baboon family was gathering for this happy occasion, and as if they were waiting for their invitation.

Annie and Sienie hooked onto either side of me as I got out of the car and took me by the arm to our egg-room. This cooling facility was neat. It was the pride of the farm. No one was allowed to enter the area without following the strict disinfectant rules that Sienie had implemented. I would enjoy no exception.

"Here is our first shipment. Ready to go," Annie said. Like sparkling white pearls, the tops of the cleaned eggs were sticking out from their packing boxes. "One thousand two hundred eggs, brother Yan," Sienie proudly said. "Just as you ordered them. They are ready to leave tomorrow."

For a moment, even I, as tired as I was, could not help but to get excited. "Twelve hundred eggs, times $350.00 each!" Wow, at last, we're ready to move with much more comfort.

Annie opened the large Incubator doors for me to look inside. "Look, they're full also. We're expecting our first hatch soon, and the fertility rate of these eggs were all over 90%," she proclaimed proudly.

These two sisters were like little excited children. The months of hard work and tension were finally over. I knew they were looking at me as their hero, and their world was fulfilled. Mine was so far away.

As I stepped out of the egg-room, I noticed a few dark clouds on the horizon and for a brief moment I thought I saw a bolt of lightning. A threatening vice-like feeling gripped my spirit as I remembered the two followers outside the department of Wildlife. "I wonder what those two are up to?"

Our black African workers had gathered themselves next to the fires in two neat rows. They were dressed in their neat blue and white outfits, with their white caps and matching white boots. When African people are happy, they sing and dance. My workers waited for me to step outside, and then they sang, and they danced. Their voices blended together in perfect harmony, like only the African people can do. They were singing about the white man who came from America and gave them food and shelter. Their feet announced a perfect beat and the fires were burning. I felt Africa under my feet. For a brief moment I became one with the dancers. The melody of their sweet song caused great satisfaction in my spirit. My people were happy but I was wondering why I was not?

My sisters with their families were standing to one side, and they were happy. I noticed Sienie's glance towards me. She smiled but I knew she could feel that my heart was not there.

Sienie was born with a sixth sense. I had always believed that she could sense trouble ten miles away. She had the uncanny ability to always come and stand at my right shoulder and whisper certain warnings or words of advice into my ear.

Today was no different. While everyone else was in a festive spirit, Sienie came up like a shadow to my side, and whispered: "My Boetie, you know that I trust you, but I do not trust the President or any of his people. Something is drastically wrong. Please move carefully."

I did not wish to alarm her or anyone else at this time, by agreeing with her, so I forced a smile and said: "Don't worry Sis, I have things under control.

Ever since the visit of the President, the same eerie feeling had gotten a hold of me, and would not let go.

I lifted my eyes over the dancing, singing figures and looked toward the North. I wanted to go home. A lightning bolt brought me back to reality. There was a storm coming, but it seemed to be heading somewhere else first...

"SATAN" MEETS HIS MATCH

Keeping other animals out of contact with the Ostriches was a real challenge for us, since this was one of the requirements of the USDA for any of the birds that were involved in exports to the USA.

These requirements are very necessary to keep diseases of all kinds away from the United States.

A very expensive eight-foot fence was put in place around the entire perimeter, with a twenty-two thousand volt electric line alongside it, at the top, on the bottom and in the middle.

This electric line was most definitely the only way to keep night scavengers out. Although the Ostriches were more than capable to stand their ground against most of these animals, leopards, lions and hyenas would be a different thing.

Elephants would not intentionally go into the camps, but if they developed an itch, which is often the case, it would not be impossible for them to lean on one of the posts for a scratch and then push the entire fence line down.

In spite of the electric line, we had all sorts of warning devices in place to alert us to any form of entry.

Any slight interference in these camps caused the birds to drop in production. We could not afford any interference, so, nothing was left over to coincidence if it could be helped.

The way things had been going, we also realized that the slightest issue would be enough to get the Botswana Veterinarian on our backs.

We were not taking any chances. Our farm, with all the exportable birds, and coupled with the quarantine station in the USA were incredibly valuable.

Only a few days after our initial USDA inspection, a Corporation in the USA offered us twenty million dollars for our business.

We were not ready to sell, but soon this was going to be the thing to do. The matter was already discussed in detail between the partners and, agreed upon.

Outside our backyard, the kopje[3] offered haven to a large troop of baboons. They would often offer great entertainment to the folks on the farm when they would get involved in family feuds, or parents applying discipline to the kids.

Every now again, they had to be scared off when they would become to sure of themselves in Annie's vegetable garden or trying to get into the Ostrich pens.

Baboons loved to eat eggs, and these Ostrich eggs were such a challenge for them. Every now and again, one of them would take on the challenge of trying to climb the electric fence, and it would be so funny to watch him react when he would get an enormous electric shock.

---

[3] A Kopje is the difference between a hill and a mountain.

The noise at that moment would echo through the kopje, and the rest of the troop would join in a combined chorus as they all lamented the misery of the victim.

The laborers in the yard would laugh and cheer as such a baboon would run away with his tail high up in the air behind him, and showing his teeth towards us as if to say: "I will get you one of these days."

The high voltage lines carried very little amperage and therefore would not kill, but it certainly did get their attention.

For several days, such a brave baboon would not come anywhere close to the fence, but then after a few days, the desire for one of the eggs would bring him back again, until we finally were left with no alternative but to fire on such a baboon with a rifle.

What seemed to be one of the leaders of the troop, was starting to give us a real hard time. Somehow, the beast had discovered a way to get into the camps and then steal or break the eggs.

The rest of the troop would mock and bark at us from the kopje, as if they had won a mighty battle.

Several times, the men on the farm accepted the challenge to try in vain to get this large baboon with the .303 rifle. This leader of the troop would position himself in a tree over in the distance after his exploits in our camps, and then bark his open disgust at us.

As if he knew he was too far too be shot down, he would sit and bark at the men even after several attempts to shoot him down. When one of the shots would get too close for comfort, he would climb down at his leisure and then move to a different spot when he was ready and continued his mockery.

Johannes named him "Satan," because he said: "No one can get to him and he steals and he robs." The name stuck and everyone started referring to this Baboon as satan.

This baboon was indeed worthy of his name. He robbed, stole, destroyed and it seemed as if he was immune to all our attempts to get him out of our world.

Bertus took the old .303 rifle, which belonged to our neighbors and in his normal calm and collective manner, spent several hours setting the sights.

He was as tired of satan as everyone else on the farm. "Enough is enough," he told one of the workers. "We will show that baboon who is boss of this farm." He smiled, but he was determined that satan was not going to show us off anymore.

It was hard to get a license to keep a rifle on the farm. Our friendly neighbor told us that as little as we had need of the thing, he would not mind if we borrowed it from time to time. All that we needed to do was to purchase our own shells.

Word about satan running loose on our farm spread to the neighbors, and every time we came together, one more joke would be added to the list of previous ones.

The neighbors knew that I was a preacher and this made the joke even more interesting.

"Other preachers would get satan with the Word, but Yan cannot even get him with a .303 rifle," was one of the favorite teases, even though I had not even taken aim at the animal yet.

"Well, don't you think it is time YOU take aim at your enemy," the neighbor asked, after I tried to jokingly defend myself.

The next morning, one of the workers came and showed us again a few broken eggshells left behind in one of the camps by satan.

"We chased satan, but he is there in the tree, barking at us right now." The worker pointed up the kopje with his pointed finger at the end of an outstretched arm.

Dries was on the farm visiting, and he grabbed the rifle, loaded a few shells into it, and went outside. Everyone gathered at the gate where Dries took dead aim and fired, but satan remained seated and coughing baboon curses at us.

Manie took his turn, and hit the branch next to satan. In his normal easy manner, he climbed down from the tree, and moved a hundred yards further into the next tree. He was sitting in the open, about six hundred yards away.

"Give me that rifle Manie," I said, and everyone cheered. The neighbor's wife was standing in the small crowd, and teased me by saying: "Do you think you can still shoot straight?" Everyone laughed, but I didn't. I was taking this matter serious. Even though it was a baboon, and not really the devil himself, I saw this as some sort of a spiritual challenge.

"Reckon, where do you want the shot?" I asked the kind little lady from next door.

"Only a head shot or one into the heart of the enemy will be accepted from a man of God like you," she teased me back.

Several of the African workers were standing around. Bertus was down in one of the camps, and would have liked to try the newly adjusted rifle for himself, but there was no way we could wait for him.

I took care and adjusted the open site to six hundred yards. I was amazed at the tension I felt to live up to the challenge of bringing satan down. I took a deep breath. Silence fell over the little crowd. Everyone had his or her eyes on the target. The arrogant satan was sitting sideways from me. Even at this distance, he had a commanding appearance.

The loud bang of the old .303 rifle rang out and she kicked hard against my shoulder when I pulled the tender trigger. Satan fell forward and the African people danced with joy. Dries smiled and jokingly said, "He is moving to another tree."

Johannes stood next to me and with admiration in his eyes said: "He is dead Bwana, you killed satan. You want me to go and fetch him?" I nodded, and Johannes, accompanied by another

74

Pikaneen,[4] set off to fetch what he believed to be the dead satan.

Everyone waited at the gate for the two men to return. After a while they appeared out of the brush, carrying ol' satan between the two of them.

He was one of the biggest baboons I had ever seen in all my life.

The shot entered his left ear and came out the other. It was a perfect shot. One of the best I had ever attempted.

The Africans sang a victory song that day, of the Maruti,[5] that killed satan. Did I feel proud? Yes, I would have to lie if I did not, but then I said to myself with a smile, "I wish it was that easy," as I walked back to the house for a cup of tea.

---

[4] A descriptive word for a young, black African boy

[5] Marutti is the African name for Preacher in that part of the Continent

ANNIE IS SICK

The whole night I had been fighting off the blitz attacks of hungry mosquitoes. I must have turned a hundred times in my bed, listening to the sounds outside and waiting for the day to break so that we could get the first shipment off and I could then go home.

Hyena's snooped around the yard most of the night and the call of a lonely jackal in the distance was often answered by several others around the yard, waiting their turn for the remains of last night's festivities. I was wondering why one of them decided to stay in the distance? Why not come and join the rest of the scavengers?

Finally, the first call of the turtledove reminded me that the day had finally arrived, and the crickets outside stopped their monotonous choir attempt.

The smell of a fresh pot of coffee brought me to my feet and even though the sun was not out yet and it was only five in the morning, I decided to wake the rest of the house with a fresh cup "We need to get an early start, I want to get home" I said cheerfully. Everyone knew that my heart was no longer there on the farm.

"Did you hear the hyenas last night?" I asked as I walked into Annie and Bertus' room. "Ja," Bertus answered in his Afrikaans language. "We did not sleep much. Annie is not well. We need to get her to a doctor soon." This little sister of mine was suffering from cancer in the bladder. For two years it seemed as if the doctors had the problem under control with chemotherapy treatment, but now I was disturbed to learn that she was once again in much pain and bleeding.

Around the breakfast table, Annie was sitting with an expression of pain but would know nothing about staying in bed or about taking the long road to the Republic of South Africa where she could see her doctors in Johannesburg. "Just say a prayer for me please." All eyes immediately turned to me, and I knew that they expected me to take the lead. They knew me as "the man of God." What they did not know was that a few days ago I tried to find the Father, to hand him back this wrench, but I could not find Him.

Together we cried out to the Lord, and the place was filled with a spirit of expectancy. I prayed an emotional prayer and my words touched their hearts, but I was aware that God did not come. He was still so far away from me, and it felt as if I was on an island all alone.

Looking back today, I know that I should have stopped everything and first tried to find my way back to the Lord. But like so many of us I thought that I would find Him up front somewhere again. What I did not know was that the path I was on continued on in a direction directly opposite from my best Friend. The storm up ahead would turn my way, and once it did, the onslaught would be fierce. It would be destructive and strong enough to uproot and destroy me unless God intervened.

Outside the dogs started barking, which meant that the workers were arriving. Annie would know nothing about staying in bed, and insisted to do her part, filling out the dozens of export forms and having them ready when the Botswana Veterinarian would arrive for his final inspection.

Johannes, one of our most faithful workers, stood in front of my office with his hat in his hand. A typical African custom, indicating that he wanted to talk with me.

"Yes, Johannes," I said after I stepped outside with him. "Bwana, I saw something on the Kopje yesterday." He paused and I knew he wanted me to invite him to carry on with the news. This was their custom. The listener had to show enough interest, and then the man would proceed with the detail. "Wait a minute Johannes," I said, and walked over to the kitchen. I came out with two soft drinks and headed over to the shade of the big tree in the back yard. Johannes followed me, and sat down with me as we drank our soda together. We talked about the weather first, and then about his kids.

Finally I said: "So, your sharp eyes saw something up there?" He indicated so with his head and then told me that he saw movement half way up the hill the day before. "Did you investigate what it was?" He nodded his head again, and explained how he went up there from the back of the hill the day before. "Hau,[6] I saw two white men with binoculars sitting there, watching the people on the farm." He explained to me what they looked like, and was real proud to make me understand that they did not see him. "Bwana, you want to go up there with me?" I shook his hand, and said: "Well done Johannes.

---

[6] Their way to express amazement

Yes, I do.   Let's just get our work done here first.
Don't tell anyone about it yet."

As Johannes walked away with his cap now back
on his head, I could not help but experience that
eerie feeling once again, knowing that even now,
I was being watched closely.

"What was going on here?" I asked myself out
loud as I walked back to the rest of the crew.   I
decided that I was going to climb that Kopje
today, and those two men would have some
explaining to do.

Annie was filling out the forms, but I could see
that she was not feeling well.

"Father, where are you?   I need your
guidance..."

HERE WE GO

Every one was tired. The first shipment was hard work. Cleaning and packing twelve hundred ostrich eggs was no joke.

The State Veterinarian arrived and from the outset it was evident to all that he was going to make it as difficult as possible for us.

I remembered him from a few weeks before. He was present when the USDA approved our farm. He was also there when the president's farm was not approved...

All the eggs had to be unpacked. He had to see each one. The packing material was not to his liking and then the way that the labels were done also did not meet his arrogant approval.

The eggs were suppose to be flown to the airport, but for days it had been raining and the airstrip were too soggy for the pilot to land the twin-engine aircraft.

Urgent ground transportation had to be arranged, and as we packed them into the back of the truck, the Veterinarian even had some complaint about the type of truck we were using.

All this time he carried a sneer on his face and the only thing we could do was to dance according to his tune.

The festive spirit of last night was no longer there. Men and women were working at a relentless pace. We only had a certain time to make it to the border. They closed at four in the afternoon, and this spiteful Veterinarian tried his best to stretch things as late as possible.

When the driver finally started the truck a few minutes before three thirty, men and women forgot their weariness. The excitement was back. A cheer went up which reminded me of the times when Tiger Woods would make a difficult golf-shot appear so easy. This was not an easy shipment and when the truck finally pulled out, the Veterinarian stood there as the loser, looking at the truck as if to say, "Well, I tried my best shot, but just could not win."

"Johannes," I cried out to the man who told me about the two spies outside the hill. "Come, let's go and pay a visit to those two men and see if they can tell us why they don't come to the house for coffee."

Johannes smiled, and immediately started walking out in front of me. We walked out of site first, around the kopje, so that when we climbed up on the steep side, we would not be seen. This side of the kopje was very steep and dangerous to climb. A steep cliff on that side, challenged our moves, but there was no other way to do it.

I was not in a good mood. I knew that I would step heavily on those two men today. There was some explaining to do, and I was not going to tolerate their arrogance, which they displayed before. "They were now trespassing on our property and that is the end of the matter."

Careful not to make any noise, we climbed over the dangerous cliff-side of this little mountain. I was surprised at the agility of Johannes. You could not hear a sound from him, and I was careful to follow in his steps every inch of the way.

"Let me just catch my breath first Johannes." I had to stop him because he was ready to move forward immediately after we reached the top. I had already decided that he was obviously much more physically fit than I.

The prowling skills of this young Botswana man impressed me. You could not hear a sound coming from him as we moved forward, even though there was much dry brush all around.

While I was following Johannes, I was thinking about what I was going to do when I found these two men up there.

This was not the right time to get on my wrong side. I was not in a good mood. In fact, I was in a fighting mood, and although I was telling myself to act mature about this, I realized that one wrong word from either of the two men would spark me into a violent response. "Enough is enough. Today, this thing will end."

Johannes moved more carefully now, and I told myself that we must be close to their position. I could now see the house beneath, and the workers moving around in the yard.

Suddenly, Johannes started talking out loud. "They are not here Bwana." He pointed to a place where they had been camping out. The signs that they had been there, were visible all around. Several cigarette stumps were lying all around. It did not appear as if they had a tent there, but the place where their bedrolls were placed, was visible. The remains of a fire told me that they could not have left there too long ago, as the ashes were still hot.

I was irritated and felt the tension inside me mount up. "We will come again Johannes. I want you to check this place out regularly and when you see them, let me know right away."

I marked the place in my mind. I knew exactly what I would do the next time. I was going to scare the living daylights out of them.

"Now, I had to get to the border gate first. We had a shipment of eggs to get through, and by the looks of it, we had all sorts of enemies trying to stop us."

CHAPTER 3

THIS THING HAS NO ENDING

"OH, SAY, CAN YOU SEE?"

The scrumptious meal in the business class section of Air France was delightfully good. I finally stretched my feet forward and pushed the reclining section of the seat backward so that I could relax my stressed out body.

The movie did not interest me, so I set the mask that they provided over my eyes and laid back. Right now, I was enjoying the flight back to my country.

"It has been just too long mister," I told the friendly customs official when he asked how long I was in Botswana.

The only time I could make any contact with my family by phone was the rare times that I would go into town. We had done everything we could, to get a phone on the farm, but without any success. The normal bribes did not work that time.

I could not help but think how different it would have been if we had taken the President in as a partner.

There was just no way I could convince Manie about this though. Manie just did not trust the man, and nothing I could do, short of demanding it, could convince him.

"We made a terrible mistake, that is for sure." I smiled at myself after saying this. These last few months, I had learned to talk to myself. It was so funny, because I never used to do this. I find people staring at me, as I am having a full conversation and no one is with me. "This business is driving me crazy, that is for sure." I looked over to my left, and the passenger next to me smiled. I smiled back at him and shrugged my shoulder shyly.

At Jan Smuts Airport in Johannesburg, everything went so smoothly. No questions were asked. All the paper work was in order and I was told that Annie did a fabulous job, filling out all the documents.

I left her behind sick. Bertus was going to take her to the hospital the next day, and I could not help but to give her an extra hug when I left for Johannesburg. She smiled through some tears and told me to give Elizabeth a hug for her.

"Bring me something nice from America," she said as I left her. I smiled when she asked this because she knew that I never came back to the farm without bringing all of them something from home. I loved to spoil them because they were all so loyal and hard working. To me, they were like my little children who got excited every time I came home. The first thing they did when I arrived in Botswana was to wait around my luggage until I opened it up and presented them with the gifts. Elizabeth knew what to send the ladies, and for the men, I always had a nice tool of sorts.

It took serious self-control from all of us at the Botswana border gate, because when we got there with the shipment of eggs, they were not in a hurry to help us. When they finally started, they decided that the truck had to be offloaded.

It was very obvious to all of us that these custom officials at the border gate were working in cahoots with the enemy, and they did everything possible to harass us in every possible way.

Outside the sun was scourging the earth with over one hundred degree temperature and with the truck standing still, the heat was building up fast inside the truck, which was not good for the eggs.

"The seal that I put on the back door of this truck cannot be removed by anyone other than the officials at Jan Smuts Airport, and if you do, the eggs can be trashed, because they will not reach America," the State Veterinarian told us when we left the farm.

I had no way to prove this, but when the Veterinarian arrived at the gate "for a beer", as he stated it, his timing messed up the plans of the border patrol officials. His obvious intention was not to drink a beer, but to come and enjoy our frustration when the truck would be turned back.

However, now after arriving when he did, he had no alternative but to substantiate what we told them about not offloading the truck, and we finally were allowed through.

When you look at most countries on the Continent of Africa, you can understand why they are in the state they find themselves in. Reason and regulations are non-existent. Everyone does as he pleases. Each man with a slight advantage over another does not mind to demonstrate it and any process is slowed as much as they can.

Nothing in Africa comes easy when left in the hands of bureaucrats. These power-crazed individuals will do everything possible to make you understand that they have the power in their hands. Very few of them display any form of humanity. If you do not have patience, Africa is not the place to be in.

Slowly, the long awaited sleep overtook me in the Aircraft, and I drifted away into a land of peace. I dreamed about the cliff we were climbing. I suddenly slipped and Johannes grabbed me by the hand, but then his grip started slipping and just as I fell the voice of the Pilot came over the air, announcing that we were preparing the descent for our arrival in Los Angeles. I was so glad to be out of that dream.

When my fellow passenger noticed that I was awake, he leaned over to me and with a smile said: "You don't only talk to yourself when you are awake, but you are also very talkative in your sleep."

We laughed and I told him that I had a lot to talk about. We laughed and started talking about the political scene in the United States. He had several good things to say about President Clinton, and after we landed he started singing the National Anthem. I stared through the window at the land, which I had grown to love so much.

"Thank you Father, for your grace and mercy," I seemingly said out loud again, because at the end of the line, my passenger friend, said "Amen." We laughed spontaneously. We were both happy to be home.

Manie had to wait his turn, and did not mind to do so, because Elizabeth was in my arms. She was crying and laughing at the same time. My two kids were waiting patiently for their turn behind her. No one was going to steal this moment from her.

"The next shipment is yours to deal with Manie," I said as I hugged this kind-hearted brother of mine. CJ, my son and Reynette, my daughter grabbed me on either side. "Oh, daddy, I missed you so much", Reynette, cried out with much emotion. "Please tell me you are not going back soon!" Though Elizabeth was not saying anything, I noticed her long look into my eyes after Reynette's comments.

"No, my darling, the next one is for CJ and Manie to handle. Mommy won't let me go soon, will you darling'?"

CJ grabbed a little flag from a newsstand and pushed it into my belt. "We have you anchored this time. You are here to stay," he grabbed my bags and said: "Dad, you and Mom get out of here. Manie and I will take care of the shipment. We have you booked into the Holiday Inn here at the airport, so you don't have to drive far."

Everyone laughed, but Elizabeth and I laughed in a different way. We laughed because we were complete. We were together and right now, we needed each other's embrace.

Six O' Clock the following morning I woke up on the seventeenth floor of the Holiday Inn. Something was amiss. At first I could not figure it out and then it dawned on me that an alarm was ringing in our room.

"What is going on honey?" Elizabeth wanted to know. We were both taking a few moments to get our thoughts together. Then it dawned on me that the building was moving in a strange way. I ran to the window, and to my horror, noticed that we were in the midst of an earthquake and we were on the seventeenth floor! The building swayed from one side to the other.

Several minutes later, we joined other guests on the sidewalk outside the building.

"Nothing in my life is normal anymore, honey." I laughed nervously as I said it, but it was so close to the truth. "Isn't there anything that can go right anymore?"

EGGS, AIRBORNE.

After almost eight years of continuous drought, all of a sudden the clouds literally tore open over Botswana. News about flooding and people cut off from civilization, reached the news in the USA.

Manie was on the farm to handle the next shipment. The next batch of eggs was sold and paid for, and had to make the airport on time. The situation was critical. Roads and bridges were washed away and there was no end in sight.

For days I did not hear from Manie, and I knew that he probably could not get to a working phone. Finally, word reached me that Barry and Annie almost drowned as they tried to cross a low water bridge. The flood washed the bridge away with them on it. The Four-wheel drive vehicle ended up in the crocodile infested waters.

Annie and Barry desperately crawled through the open windows of the vehicle and climbed to the top of it. The crazy waters rumbled and pushed passed the vehicle, trying to overturn it.

Barry shouted at Annie to make a jump for it, and even though she is a strong swimmer, she realized that the months of illness together with the strong current was going to make it impossible.

Barry was not a strong swimmer at all and he knew that both their lives were now in jeopardy.

Finally the vehicle washed up against a rock and the mad waters now washed up higher, threatening to push them off the roof of the vehicle.

One of the neighboring farmers showed up just in time. Annie realized that she could not hold on much longer. Her tired arms were loosing its grip on the side of the vehicle when suddenly a rope was thrown for her to grab onto.

As soon as she let go of the vehicle to grab the rope, her hands slipped and the next minute she washed off the vehicle and was swept away with the current.

Pandemonium broke loose now. Sienie and Bertus had now also arrived on the scene and before Bertus could stop her, she also jumped into the river screaming, "I'm coming Annie, I'm coming."

Bertus realized that he had to keep control of his senses. With one sweep of his hand, he grabbed the rope from the neighbor's hand and stayed on the embankment, running to keep up with Annie.

Only one hundred yards further, the water would wash into a large, calm area, but Bertus realized that this is where the crocodiles would be congregating and both the ladies were on their way there.

Sienie was now struggling to stay alive. Cramps in her legs and hip threatened to draw her under, when suddenly she managed to grab onto a tree branch, which was stuck in the water.

The exhausted Annie was hardly fighting anymore and washed passed the tree. Bertus realized that he had only one chance left to save his wife.

This muscular South African planted himself on a rock by the side of the water. His strong arms swung the lifeline above his head and with adrenalin rushing through his body, he released the rope with every ounce of his strength and shouting at the top of his lungs for her to grab onto it.

Even still today, Bertus will tell you that he is convinced that Angels carried that rope right in front of the tired Annie. The loop, which Bertus made in front of the rope, almost fell over her head.

Annie realized that this was the final moment. Visions of her two children and her precious grand children filled her mind and caused her to take a strong breath of fresh air, unwilling to give up this fight, when she felt the rope on top of her and the voice of her husband shouting.

With the last ounce of her strength she pushed her head and one arm through the loop and the rope tightened.

The strong South African pulled the rope over his shoulder and without any hesitation he walked up the embankment, pulling his wife to safety.

Sienie is a skinny but stubborn, frail fighting machine. She not only held on for dear life, but she was still trying to cry out instructions to those around her, in order to save Annie. Only now with Annie safely on the shore, did she finally turn her attention back to her own self and she was also pulled to the side by other rescuers.

Barry was already on the ground and the rescuers now paid attention to the vehicle.

When news reached us about this crisis on the farm, Elizabeth came and sat on my lap. Something she always does when she has a serious matter on her heart.

"Honey, you know that I want you to stay with me as long as possible. I know however, that your heart is with the crew in Botswana. I will pack your clothes tonight, and get you a flight to South Africa in the morning."

This short little lady is only small in a physical build. She is a giant in every other way. I always tell people, that I asked God one day to see an angel. I had always heard people talking about this incredible experience. God answered my prayer, He showed me an angel, and I married her!

I am convinced that there are not too many marriages that would have lasted the continuous tests we had to face. God knew exactly what He did when He gave me Elizabeth.

I decided that there was no other answer for our problem. We will have to invest in an airplane large enough to carry these heavy boxes of eggs. For now, we solved the immediate problem by chartering a King-Air airplane.

All these arrangements were done even before I left the USA, and as I stepped into the Airport at Johannesburg, Manie and a pilot were there to meet me ready to escort me to the chartered aircraft. Time was of the essence, and we could not waste any of it.

When we planned the farm, one of the things we thought about was an airstrip. Now, it was going to pay off. No one knew we were coming, and I told the pilot to fly over the house one time to alert our people.

Sienie had just woken up and was in the bathroom. Bertus was awake but still snoozing for a few minutes longer. Annie was awake and drinking a cup of coffee when all of a sudden the incredible sound of this fast moving aircraft cut through the air. This sudden noise was so loud and fast that the coffee cup dropped from Annie's hand and spilled over the carpet. The place came alive. Somehow, Sienie knew right away that it was we.

"It is Manie. It is Manie. I tell you guys, it is he," she cried out.

Still in their pajamas, everyone jumped on the back of the little pickup in the yard, and raced towards the airstrip, just in time to see us land.

As we stepped out of the airplane, a shout of joy filled the air. "My boetie, my boetie," Sienie chanted and danced as she noticed me there also, and waited for us to step down.

"Wow," Bertus said. "You guys know how to wake people up." Manie's face was showing the stress of the past few days, but he was happy.

When he learned that I was coming to South Africa, he made sure that he was in Johannesburg to meet me. On the way to the farm, he filled me in about all the events of the past few weeks, and how they almost lost their lives.

"Yan, I tell you man, the roads are gone. There is just no way that we can transport the eggs on those roads, and the Government is not doing anything to make the situation better. I just do not understand how these farmers can make a living here. There is no way that the vehicles can hold up under these conditions." Manie went on to explain that the shipment was ready, and already cleared by the State Veterinarian.

"When we get back to Johannesburg today," he said, "I want to show you a beautiful Airplane that we can get for a good price. The owner of the aircraft is in financial trouble and if we make him a reasonable offer, he will take it." This is the way I know Manie. He is always ready with a new plan.

"Bwana, they're back!" I turned around to face Johannes who appeared behind me. He was half crouched, and was talking with an urgent whisper. "They are there, they are there, and I saw them. This morning I saw movement there, and when I climbed up, I saw them. They are there Bwana."

"Today, I am going to teach those men a lesson my friend." I turned and left Johannes with Manie. I walked into the house and came out with the .303 rifle.

"What's going on?" Manie wanted to know with surprise in his eyes, as he saw me head for the gate. "Bwana Yan is going to kill those two bad men up on the hill," Johannes informed Manie with glee.

"No Johannes, I am not going to kill them, but I am going to give them the scare of their lives." I briefly filled Manie in with what had been happening on that kopje.

I made sure that the rifle was loaded. I could not see the two men, so I asked Johannes: "Are they on the same spot?" Johannes nodded and then said: "Shoot them Bwana, shoot them quick."

He was not taking his eyes off the spot for one moment, and I could not help to crack a smile while I was taking aim. Johannes appeared almost bloodthirsty.

The last time I was up there, I marked a spot where a beehive was hanging from a tree just above the position where they were laying in their spying position.

As soon as the shot rang out, I thought for a brief moment that I saw movement, but then a few seconds later, the two men clearly jumped up, waved their arms and then disappeared.

"You got them Bwana, you got them good." Johannes laughed and then told Manie. "He hit the beehive. They will chase them now."

"I don't think we will see them again soon Johannes." We laughed, and turned back to the house where the others were waiting for us to join them before we would take off with the next shipment.

Bertus was in a talkative mood. Ever since we had landed on our airstrip, Bertus had been investigating the Airplane.

"Manie," he said. "That is what we need for the eggs. We need our own airplane." As if we had not thought about it ourselves, Bertus proceeded to tell us about the advantages of the airplane versus carrying the eggs on the road. Bertus is a man of great detail, but we allowed him to carry on, and Manie and I were sitting patiently, waiting for our turn to inform him of our plan to acquire the Aircraft.

Finally, Manie received his turn, and delightfully informed the little group of our future plans.

"What kind of Aircraft would this be?" Bertus asked. Manie took his time, and explained to them that it was a twin engine Aero Commander. Able to fly at thirty thousand feet, with cabin controlled pressure and fully equipped with radar and instrumentation to fly under any conditions.

"When are we going to get it?" Annie wanted to know excitedly. And for the next few minutes everyone joined in the discussions about the aircraft, like little children.

"Now Annie will be able to get to a doctor easier when she needs to." Bertus spoke out, and everyone agreed.

"By the way," Bertus looked at me and asked. "What were you shooting at a little while ago?"

Excitedly, Sienie filled all our cups with another round of coffee and with the air filled with the aroma of the fresh brew, I started telling them about these two strange and sinister looking men that have been following me since Swaziland and ended the story with the shot into the beehive.

"Good for you my boetie." Sienie grabbed my hand over the table and gave it a squeeze. "Do you think they will be back again soon?" She asked laughingly.

I assured everyone that I did not think it would be soon, but that we may have to ask Johannes to keep an eye out for us.

An hour later, we circled over the little group of workers as they waved and then that fast little King Air split the clouds on our way to Jan Smuts with the next batch of eggs.

"STEPPING UP."

The second shipment took off with no problem at all.   As soon as it was in the air, we both smiled a sigh of relief, and Manie said: "Well, it seems as if we are properly in the business now."

"Hey Manie," Someone cried out behind us on the airport.   We turned and it was a South African farmer who has been kind to us from time to time when we needed advise with our birds.

The man was standing well over six feet tall with blond hair and except for a little potbelly he was a rather good-looking man.

This kind gentleman himself was an Ostrich farmer in South Africa, and he has been keen to export some of his products to the United States, but because of the South African ban, was unable to do so.

"Do you have time for coffee?" he asked after Manie introduced me to him.   We walked over to a little corner table in a nearby Restaurant.

"How are things going with the export business?" He sincerely enquired from Manie.

"Well, we have just sent off our second shipment, and things are going great so far."   Manie spent a few minutes explaining to him about our problems with the roads and I noticed that he deliberately did not mention anything to this friendly man about our concerns with the Botswana Government officials.   I thought Manie was doing right, so I left the entire conversation over to him.

Finally the friendly farmer leaned forward over the table and looked us both in the eyes. "You and your brother should get your hands into the South African market also." He explained that with the change of power, when Mandela takes over, policies with regards to the Ostrich business may change, and if it does, we will have something going here already.

"I know of a man close to where you guys are, near Ellisras in the Northern Transvaal. He has some property that is lying empty and will be ideal for you guys to get going on. "If it was me," he said "I would get started there and purchase eggs here in South Africa, to incubate them."

He could see that he had Manie and I in close attention, so he continued. "I can help you guys with some eggs, but there is another person in the Northern Cape that will be delighted to sell his eggs to you. We are greatly upset here in South Africa that it is only the Namibian farmers who can get their eggs exported to the USA."

For the first time, I joined in the discussion and asked him: "Sir, we appreciate your advice, and I agree that you are right, but what do you get out of this?"

The man smiled and said: "Right now, nothing, but if this thing works out and the market does open here in the Republic, then I will hope that you will remember me also."

He stretched his long legs out from under the table and crossed them. The muscles showed clearly where the shorts ended, and I could not help but to think that he possibly used to be a Rugby player in his younger days. He looked as if he could have been fast. He was maybe a Center or possible a Wing, I continued to speculate in my mind.

I was brought back to reality as I heard him utter a warning to Manie and I.

"Let me warn you and your brother though," he said. "You have no idea how tight this business is controlled, and I have heard your names mentioned in certain circles that I do not trust. Be very careful, and watch your back at all times. Believe me, you cannot rule anything out from these men. They will stop at nothing."

After we parted ways, I looked over to Manie and asked him what he thought about the man's warning. Manie assured me that he also felt that we were open targets, as we were obviously taking a big bite from the Ostrich market, and these men were starting to feel threatened.

We headed over to Rand Airport on the western side of Johannesburg. We had a meeting with the owners of the Aero Commander Aircraft.

The Airplane was in perfect condition. The owner explained that the only thing he was concerned about was the fact that it wasn't flown regular enough, and that we needed all the seals checked. He also felt that it would not be a bad idea to have it submitted for a major checkup before we started using it.

The deal was closed quickly and Manie and I became the proud owner of a twin engine Airplane, paid for in cash!

The owners of the hangar where the airplane was kept agreed to have their staff do a major service for us on the aircraft and explained that it will be ready in two weeks.

"Just make sure it has everything in the right place," I said jokingly, not knowing how important my request would prove in the weeks to come.

We had no idea how close we had come to one of the major chapters in this saga when our lives would come close to being snuffed out.

BECOMING FRIENDS WITH THE DETECTIVE.

When Abraham made the offer to Lot, to make the selection of the land that he wanted, the bible says that Lot chose *for himself* all the Jordan valley, and went on his way.

He never consulted the Lord. He looked at what appeared to be right and went on his way Eastward. God would ultimately destroy the place, and Lot's influence on Sodom and Gomorrah would prove to be zero.

I knew this, and had preached it many times, but at this crucial time in my life, I became guilty of the same lack of discretion. Without consulting God, one decision after another was made. If the thing looked right, I would go ahead and do it.

The friendly blond farmer from the Airport put a thing in our minds and we set off to Ellisras in the Northern Transvaal to check out the land, he referred us to.

The place was equipped with Ostrich pens, a house, outbuildings and a very reasonable rent.

A few days later Manie and I acquired a used incubator, which we purchased immediately and sent it off to the little farm we leased for the purpose of getting our foot in the door in South Africa.

Nothing went smoother than this arrangement and within a short time, it seemed as if everything would fall into place.

When we got back to Johannesburg, a close relative informed me of an important telephone call that came in for us.

"He said his name was Piet," she told me. "He said he was a detective and that you knew him well."

I knew right away whom she was talking about. Piet was indeed a good friend of long ago, and I hadn't seen him in several years. Piet, a strong and very intelligent man, never makes a phone call in vain. Even though he was a friend, there was no way that he would try and track me down for no reason at all.

A phone call to him confirmed my suspicions. Piet got straight to the point and told me that he had serious information about Manie and me that certainly would interest us. "You need to come and see me right away, Yan." He was insistent and would not even know about meeting us for lunch the following day.

"Today brother. Today, and not a day later, I need to see you. The safest will be for you to come to my house, and make sure that you are not followed."

When I heard the words "Safe" and "followed", my interest was caught immediately.

The incident with the two "followers" on the farm jumped into my mind at that moment. I was sure that I did not hit any of them.

During my involvement in the Rhodesian war, I was rated as a sharpshooter. If there was anything I knew how to use, it was a rifle. Yet, still in my mind, I had a vice-like feeling grip me in my stomach.

After getting the address from the detective friend, Manie and I set off for our appointment with him. On the way there, I filled Manie in about the conversation on the phone. Our eyes were scanning the world around us, and a few times I made a few sudden turns to make sure that no one was following us.

Our lives had become like a Hollywood story. The word "Mafia" was only something that we heard about. Now it was becoming a reality. Death was constantly in our backdoor.

Finally we drove into the driveway of this old friend. Piet was an up and coming detective in the South African Police. The political climate however, gave reason for him to break away from the department, and he subsequently started a successful, private eye agency on his own.

He maintained contact with his friends in high circles, and worked in close proximity with the Police force when it suited him.

This muscular man with the scruffy looking beard hugged me like a bear. Dressed in the familiar khaki outfit with shorts and long socks, Piet was a striking figure with his black hair and Cape accent.

He was genuinely happy to see me. He slapped Manie hard on the back after shaking his hand at my introduction and then walked briskly into his humble home expecting us to follow him. Two vicious looking dogs followed us all the way to the front door and I was glad that Piet was there to control them.

One of the bull terrier dogs was sniffing suspiciously around me and Manie made sure that he stepped into the house before me. I harbor no fear for dogs, but these bull terrier dogs make me feel uneasy.

His office was filled with a great variety of photos, which proudly displayed his many exploits as a detective. Many gadgets of all sorts were visible in his office and it was obvious that he was deeply involved in the business of wire-tapping.

"You must be wondering what made me contact you?" Piet asked proudly. "Well, we are, but at the same time I am wondering how you managed to contact me at my Niece's house?"

Piet threw his head back, and laughed loudly. "I am Piet the detective, am I not?" He smiled and then looked at me. I knew that the man was waiting for a complimentary comment. I obliged and Piet continued to tell me about his contacts in the underworld as well as in the top brass of the South African Police.

He stretched himself out, kicked his feet on top of his messy desk, and with his arms folded behind his head, looked steadfastly at me and boldly stated: "Your life is in danger my friend. Not only you, but Manie also."

I did not even pretend to be curious now. Both Manie and I sat up straight. We were all ears.

For the second time in as many days, we were told the same thing. Our lives were in danger!

I felt anger rise up and a willingness to fight my way through.

"How do you mean our lives are in danger?" Manie asked him as if he did not understand the word "danger."

Piet ignored his question and continued to tell us that we have ruffled the feathers of some important men in the Ostrich circles.

"You have no idea what kind of people you are facing as enemies Yan. They have two 'grease-punks' on your trail almost all the time. They know everything they need to know about your business ventures and believe me; you are not up to the task of defending yourself against them. You are dealing with professionals who are hired by very rich individuals. Your life means nothing to these men.

For the next few minutes Piet explained to us about some of the acts of these men and how cruel they could be. He also explained to us that they have important Government officials on their bankroll.

"This is Mafia in its cruelest reality my friend." Piet stated while his eyes pierced ours for any response.

"Let me tell you how much I know about you and Manie, and for the next few minutes Piet astounded both of us with his accurate knowledge about our business. He knew about my visit to Namibia months ago. He also knew about some of the names of farmers I contacted, my dealings with the Swaziland, Mr. Themba, and the subsequent defeat there.

He told us about the concern these men have about the airstrip on our farm.

He mentioned Mike Englesaki and the subsequent sale of the business to us. He explained to us that Mike was not very popular with the President after selling out to us.

"One thing I must tell you. I cannot understand that you were so stupid to say 'NO' to the State President of Botswana. That was bold, but my friend, that was incredibly stupid."

I looked over to Manie, but he was as stunned as I. For a little while longer, Piet continued to share more with us, until I asked him, where he got this information.

"I told you that I have my contacts brother. When I heard your name mentioned, and I heard that this man was a preacher from America, I said to myself, it can only be my friend, Yan."

His feet suddenly came off the desk. He leaned over to me and quietly said. "Yan, I hope you understand how serious this thing really is!"

Piet listened as I told him about my encounters with the two men and how it all ended on the farm when I threw those bees down on them. Piet laughed, but then he stopped abruptly when he said: "You have a small war on your hands my friend, and I don't know how you will get through it."

"If you want my help, I will make myself available. I cannot work for free, but I will charge you only for the actual expenses and time I spend on the job."

At his request, we told him about all that we were involved in. We told him about the friendly Blonde farmer we met at the airport. Piet surprised us once again, when he pulled a file on the man. I know about him also. He is also in disfavor with this mafia group.

"Be careful from now on how and where you move here in South Africa. If I can advise you, please don't let anyone know about your plans to get started here in South Africa. That will be catastrophic. Keep it a state secret."

The man had his ears to the ground, that was for sure. It was scary to see how visible our lives were in the circles of these fearless characters.

The next day Piet arrived at our Niece's house to come and check the phone for any bugs. An hour later, he arrived proudly with the news that his suspicions were correct. The phone was indeed bugged, but he explained that if he removed it, the enemy would know. "From now on, you do your business from a payphone. If you don't mind someone listening in, continue to use this phone." All of this felt like a dream, not reality.

While Piet was talking, I realized that we were so fortunate to have him as a friend and not an enemy. The man knew his job that was for sure.

UP, AND AWAY...

As they pulled our Aircraft from of the hangar for Manie and me to see, we could not help but to feel proud.   She was ours and she was a thing of beauty.

With the seats out, we could easily load four hundred eggs at a time inside her.

We hired a good pilot who would fly for us. Delville was rated all the way from Jet fighters to Commercial Airliners.   The man was good! He was somewhere in his thirties and very excited to work for us.

"Can we visit the farm today?" Manie asked the pilot.   "Sure, give me until two this afternoon." This suited us fine because we wanted to invite our sister and brother in law in Johannesburg to be the first guests on our newly purchased aircraft and this would be a fine treat for them.

As long as I live I don't think I will ever forget the scene in the living room of our sweet sister and brother in law, when we walked in there to go and invite them "for the ride."

My sister Adrie is a year and a half younger than me, and her husband, Bernie, is one of the nicest men around.   He is a Jew, and we grew up together.   Both of us studied at the same college and graduated a year in between.

Bernie was busy watching a movie on TV. Adrie, my sister, was quietly sitting next to her husband knitting a sweater of sorts.   It was a typical scene of serenity until we walked into the room.

Bernie, is partly adventurous, but at times displays a side of fear that he prefers others not to know about. He is very suspicious of the unknown, and easily gets freaked out with bugs of any kind. He loves the outdoors, but is not comfortable at all when strange critters are crawling around him.

It took all the convincing powers that both Manie and I possessed to get them to accept our kind invitation for a visit to our farm.

"Just think about it Bernie," Manie said in a sweet tone of voice. "Tonight, you will sit on the farm around a huge campfire and barbeque some thick Ostrich steaks."

Reluctantly he turned to Adrie and told her to pack an overnight bag. "You promise me, that you will have us back here tomorrow, don't you?"

"You have our word Bernie," I assured them and Manie nodded his head in a friendly agreement. Adrie still wasn't at peace, but tried to hide her fears as she got into the car with us.

"I get nauseous rather quick Yan," she said, but then Bernie took over the discussion and calmed her fears by saying: "Lovey, you don't have to be afraid. It looks like a nice day and I think you will enjoy the flight."

Proudly, Manie and I stood there as they pulled the newly polished Aircraft around for the pilot to do all his preflight checks. As if we knew what he was doing, Manie and I walked around with the man, checking everything with him, and kicking a tire here and there.

Bernie and Adrie were standing around the Aircraft. She had a little worried look on her face, but he settled down to the idea that this would be a safe flight, since he was witness to the fact that the aircraft was just now released to us from a major service. He had also spoken to Delville and satisfied himself that the pilot was well rated for this Airplane.

One of the service men walked up to me and said: "There were two men here earlier, enquiring about you. They said they would be back. It seemed as if they knew you very well. They looked inside the airplane. I hope you don't mind"

Cold hands immediately gripped me on the inside, and Manie and I both looked at each other with concern. We remembered Piet's warning from a few days ago.

I walked back to Delville who was busy checking things under the opposite wing. "Delville, will you please make double sure about everything on the aircraft," I asked him politely. "We have a few people that would like to see us dead, and they said that precaution is better than cure." I made sure that I said it out of the hearing of Bernie and Adrie.

"Let me tell you something Yan. When I do my preflight checks, I do it as if it is my last flight. I take no chances, so relax. We will be ok, as soon as I say we are."

The man was efficient and I knew right away that I could relax. There was nothing to worry about.

"We are in good hands," I said to Manie," and walked over to Bernie and Adrie. She was starting to smile now.

The powerful jet engines on the aircraft lifted us off the airstrip with exceptional ease, and as I was sitting in the co-pilot's seat, I was impressed while I was watching the altimeter move up quickly, and at no time at all, we were nineteen thousand feet above the ground, waiting for air control to give us permission to climb up to twenty-five thousand feet.

The tension in all of us released and it was not long before we had forgotten the thoughts of alarm and everyone was enjoying himself or herself. The flight was smooth once we climbed above the clouds. In the distance were several large cumulus clouds looming, but the weather report gave us a clear bill and I put the thoughts of these clouds out of my mind.

"I would have preferred to have left earlier," I said to myself, "but the flight was going to take us just over an hour and a half, and that should be enough time to land before dark."

For a while Manie stood behind us, excitedly listening to the good things Delville had to say about our Aircraft. The radar in front of us indicated some activity in front, but Delville was not concerned, so, neither were we.

A light snack was served and Manie acted as our host. He is a natural comedian, and for almost an hour, everyone was cracking up with laughter.

The surroundings beneath us looked unfamiliar. Delville was sitting with a map in his hand, doing navigational checks. I casually leaned over to him and said: "You know, I have been checking the terrain beneath us for familiar landmarks, but I don't see any." Delville looked over to me and said "You are correct Yan. Something is not right here. Nothing matches up on the map either. We should have been here right now," and he indicated with his finger to a landmark, close to the border.

With his finger he tapped on the compass, then on the GPS, and with a frown on his face, he looked over to me and said: "I am not getting accurate readings on either of these. Something is not right."

The crew in the back was still laughing and totally unaware of the drama that was about to unfold.

"Well, what do you suggest?" I asked Delville, deliberately abandoning the concern that wanted to get a hold of me.

"Hand me my briefcase, will you? I have a portable GPS in there. I would like to just match it with what we have here," he said as he pointed towards the instruments of our Aircraft.

As I stepped to the back to pick up his briefcase, Manie asked, how long it is going to be before we get there. "I have been looking for a landmark, but I don't see one." He said, using almost the exact words that I expressed to Delville only a few minutes earlier.

"Yeah, that is what we want to check right now. We have just been talking about the same thing." All of a sudden, the smile disappeared from Adrie's face and silence fell over everyone.

As Delville made his checks, everyone was silent. Bernie and Manie were looking over our shoulder, while Adrie was nervously clutching a plastic bag in her hand. Something she kept as an emergency measure, but till now, was not needed.

"Just as I thought," Delville spoke his thoughts out loud. When he noticed our questioning looks, he explained that we were completely off coarse.

He carefully placed the sensitive portable GPS on the dashboard of the aircraft, but after a few minutes, we hit an air pocket and the instrument fell down on top of the joystick. Broken in pieces!

"Well, now we are blind." Delville said in an irritated way. Tension mounted. For the next few minutes we tried to make radio contact with Jan Smuts Airport, but without any success.

Delville explained that the only thing left for us to do now, was to descend low enough to where we could read one of the road signs beneath, in order to find out where we were.

I looked around at Adrie. She was now using the plastic bag.

We followed a small dirt road for a while until we noticed an intersection. Delville made a daring dive, sweeping extremely low over the treetops in order to read the road sign. Adrie was throwing up bad now. I felt so sorry for her.

"Good Lord, we are in Angola," Delville cried out loudly. He had every reason to be concerned. Angola was bad news. The country had been in civil war for several years now, with rebels armed to the teeth. Earlier reports of a private aircraft being shot down came into everyone's mind at that moment. It was hot news then, and we all understood the danger that we were in.

These rebels are looking for an opportunity like this to do target practice on. We have no permission to be in their airspace. For all practical purposes we were now the enemy.

"Turn around Delville," Manie instructed the Pilot unnecessarily. "Get us out of here immediately." Delville needed no encouragement. We made a 180 and immediately climbed as high as we could. All of a sudden, the dark cumulus clouds did not look so far from us any more. These giant cloud constellations were bad news and were lurking dangerously close in front of us. One thing was for sure; you do not want to end up inside one of those.

Giant Boeing 747 airplanes fly around these giant clouds. Several of these clouds were stretching fifty thousand feet up in the sky.

Delville did not say anything, but I noticed the way he looked at these clouds, he was concerned. Our radar indicated red all over the monitor, and I knew it spelled danger.

These clouds contained severe storms inside. Hail was but one of the looming dangers, and once you land inside one of these storm clouds, the aircraft could be iced up in seconds. Without flaps, the up and down drafts would throw the aircraft into one of these suctions and spit you out of the top. If you were still alive after that, the aircraft would stand no chance of recovery, and would drop to the ground like a rock.

The atmosphere was electric now, and everyone wanted to share his or her thoughts with Delville at the same time. I turned to the passengers and on behalf of Delville, said to them: "This man is a capable pilot, and certainly more than able to fly us out of this situation. Sit back, keep your safety belts on, and leave the man alone to fly this aircraft."

Silence fell over everyone. The situation was suddenly very critical. Beneath us the surroundings were rugged and definitely no place to land. We also did not know how far we had actually flown into Angola and how long it would take us to get out of this horrible situation.

Because of the increasing cloud activity ahead of us, it started getting darker soon. None of our instruments were dependable now. We did not know in which direction we were actually flying, and for some reason, Johannesburg was not responding to Delville's persistent radio calls.

The monotonous calls of the desperate pilot were met with a persistent radio silence. Only the blare of atmospheric noise was heard.

After another hour, we had to make one more dive in the few remaining moments of light. However, after the second attempt we had to give up because there was just not enough light left to read far enough ahead, and as we passed by, the speed of the aircraft was too much for us to make out anything of significance on the ground.

We were now in serious trouble. Adrie was very sick and seriously stressed out. I felt so terribly responsible.   She and Bernie were sitting in such peace, when we walked into their home and dragged them into this situation.

We were over heavy mountain terrain now.   The lightning storm was all around us, and suddenly the last appearance of day disappeared and we were left in the dark.   Our fuel was starting to get seriously low and I could not help but to notice that Delville's right leg was shaking nervously.

I was so thankful that at least our radar seemed to function.   The entire screen was red, and every few seconds; Delville dropped the wing to the left or to the right, turning the aircraft around these monstrous constellations.

At times, the aircraft would fall several hundred feet, only to be sucked up high, the next moment, and I was surprised that the wings could actually bear this consistent abuse.

Heavy rain and hail hit the aircraft and we started to shake like a cork in the water.   It seemed as if the engines were working extra hard against the heavy winds that were now tossing us up and down and from side to side.

Manie again appeared silently behind us and for a few minutes said nothing, but then leaned over to me and whispered in my ear   "Yan, I want you to know that I have confidence in your prayers. If you feel you should pray, then please don't wait much longer."   His voice was filled with stress.

For the past several minutes I had allowed my mind to unroll the recent chapters of my life.   "Is this it?" I had asked myself over and over.   I knew I was so far out of the will of the Lord, and so many decisions had been taken without my normal way of approaching Him first. Though I had whispered a few words to the Lord every now and again during the flight, I now recognized the need for the Master to seriously intervene on our behalf.

I felt so embarrassed before the Lord. Did it have to come to this, before I would seriously seek His face again? Would God not turn His face away from me and deny me the mercy which we so desperately needed right now?

Everyone in the aircraft was watching the fast drop in the fuel gauge, until we were on the danger mark of both tanks. The relentless rain would just not let up and the winds seemed to get worse y the minute.

"Shoot straight with us Delville. How concerned are you about our situation?" I asked him outright. I could not see his facial features in the dark, but when the Pilot spoke, the stress in his voice was clearly visible. "Yan, this is a matter of life and death. We are in serious trouble my friend, and I have to be honest with you, we need a miracle, and it has to happen soon."

Suddenly the presence of the Lord filled the aircraft. For the first time in months, I felt His nearness. "Oh, what a friend we have in Jesus." I called on the name of the Lord, and openly confessed my sins of disobedience and rebellion. "God, I don't make an idle promise here right now, but as soon as I can walk away from this mess, I will. Please have mercy on us, and see us through this storm."

I realized that I was a Jonah, and feared to think how he insisted they throw him overboard so that

119

the storm would cease. I did not like the idea of being thrown overboard in the middle of this storm, but I knew that only God could save us now.

The instruction from the Lord came to my spirit like it did so many times in the past. Suddenly and crystal clear, I heard the voice in my heart: "Increase the altitude."

I told Delville what I felt should be done. He agreed and said that it made sense. He explained that we would be able to reach a little further on the radio, and should we run out of fuel, we would be able to glide further.

The engines started working harder as we climbed to a new altitude and as we reached thirty thousand feet, Johannesburg suddenly picked us up on the radio. They informed us that they could see us on their radar.

New life came into the cockpit. A cheer went up, but Delville urgently asked for silence as he tried to listen to the voice through the crackling noise of the radio.

We were told that we were a half an hour from a landing strip and Deville was told what to do. It was going to be close. The fuel situation was now more critical than before.

I was in a different world at that moment. For the first time in months I had actually heard the voice of God in my spirit again. "Wow, Master, I thought I would never hear from you again," I said softly, and tears of appreciation washed over my face. Happiness flooded my spirit, and I allowed my spirit, freedom to pray, as it wanted. My prayer language flowed over my lips, and though I realized that Delville possibly had no idea what was happening, I did not care. I laughed and cried at the same time.

The air-control tower in Johannesburg escorted us into the town of Potgietersrust where we would land. "We have problems raising someone to turn on the landing lights for you," the friendly Air Traffic Controller informed us. "Don't worry though, we will get something done by the time you get there, even if we have to get cars to light up the strip for you."

As we arrived over the town, the left engine spluttered once, but then kept on rolling a few minutes longer as we made the turn for the strip. "I will have to land this aircraft now sir," Delville told the Controller nervously. "We are now flying only on fumes."

The next minute the lights came on, and a cheer went up inside the Airplane. Delville joined in the cry of relief and then the left engine stopped! We were almost on the ground though, and it did not matter.

I took a quick glance back at the rest of the group. Bernie was holding Adrie bravely around the shoulder. Manie was sitting up straight, but appeared to be calm.

All of a sudden it was over! We were stationary on the airstrip. The engines were turned off, and it was quiet. Only the sound of rain could be heard outside. Delville sat with his head hanging. The stress must have been severe for him.

Adrie was crouching forward, still clutching the half-full plastic bag in her hand.

Finally, Delville lifted his head and said: "Wow, that was close folks. I don't know if anyone knew how close to death we all were."

Everyone nodded their head, and I knew, that they all had the same awareness, of the closeness of death.

Spontaneously I started thanking God, and I heard an "Amen" from all present. We needed a miracle, and God came through for us.

We were landed on a military airstrip and Air force officials volunteered an aircraft mechanic to check the instruments for us so that we could fly to the farm early in the morning.

Because there were no telephones on the farm, we were sure that the folks there would be beside themselves with fear and concern by now. Word was sent to them via a neighboring farmer to expect us, and now, because of the stormy weather, the phones were out again. We could not reach them.

"You go to the motel and settle down for the night. I want to spend time here with these men to find out what went wrong. I just don't believe that it could be possible for these instruments to go out of whack the way they did, straight after a major service on this aircraft," Delville said.

Everyone including myself was relieved, but tired to the bone. We did not need encouragement to go to where we could rest. I needed a cup of coffee, and I needed a bed.

THE END - OR THE BEGINNING?

The air was clean this morning after the rains. The takeoff was smooth and flying at seventeen thousand feet, there was no movement at all. Not a cloud was noticed for miles around and it seemed as if one could see forever.

The sun was hardly up when Delville came knocking on our door, waking us up with coffee in his hands.

"I don't know what is going on here Yan?" He had a worried look in his eyes and the man was not happy at all. Without waiting for an answer he continued with the next question. "When you told me yesterday that there were people trying to kill you, I wasn't taking much notice, but last night we discovered a huge magnet that someone had deliberately placed behind the dashboard amongst all the instruments on your aircraft. Who is trying to kill you?"

I pulled my feet up so that Delville could sit on the bed next to me, and then Manie and I briefed him about what Piet had told us. "I tell you Delville, this is not speculation anymore, or unfounded phobias. This is reality my friend. We are dealing with some serious criminals.

I felt anger in my spirit. This was not fair play. "You could have aimed a little lower on the farm instead of hitting the beehive," Manie jokingly said, and though we chuckled about it, I realized that this was nothing else but outright war. The only problem though, was that the enemy had all the weapons in his hands.

The atmosphere in the aircraft was solemn. No one was relaxing and a tense silence was hanging in the air.

At first Adrie did not want to get back in the airplane, but Delville assured her that he and the Aircraft Mechanic went through all the instruments and he was satisfied. "Everything was in working order," he assured this nervous sister of ours.

Just before we boarded the airplane, the Mechanic presented Delville with his own GPS instrument and said: "I am sure that everything is working good, but just to be on the safe side, take my portable unit with you. When you get to Johannesburg, please ship it back to me."

This time, very carefully, Delville was plotting out our coarse, and every couple of minutes, he would make sure that landmarks would correspond with his map. He even took out the GPS of the Mechanic and assured himself several times that the compass of the aircraft was keeping us on course. Nothing was taken for granted.

Half way to the farm, Delville turned around and looked at the nervous Adrie. "Mmm, I see you did not bring your plastic bag with you on board today. Is that a good sign or what?"

Adrie smiled and suggested jokingly that there was no need to do so, as there was nothing left in her entire system to come out. Everyone laughed and for the moment the atmosphere became less tense.

"There is our farm," Manie pointed out excitingly as we neared the final landmark, which was the kopje behind our house. Manie was sitting next to Delville in the co-pilot's seat.

On the ground, Sienie and Annie were sitting outside drinking a cup of tea, when they heard the sound of the airplane approaching. "It is them Annie, Praise God, they've made it." With that, they ran over to the outbuildings and told the men, "Let's go, Manie and Yan are here."

They were waiting for us the previous night and when we did not show up and the weather looked so bad, they said a prayer for us. Bertus assured them that Delville would have landed the aircraft somewhere safe. "He would never fly in this kind of weather."

Out of the airplane, we noticed the racing pickup with the two ladies on the back, waving at us. We waived back as if they could see us.

The tense atmosphere was gone and excitement was even visible in Adrie.

Delville, circled the airstrip to check out the wind direction, and made a wide turn as he lined up with the runway. Flaps were checked, speed was reduced and we came in for the landing.

My mind was at ease, and I thanked God that we had arrived safely. Even though Delville had assured us that everything was in order, I could not shake loose the nagging suspicion that something else could go wrong. Now for the first time, I could relax.

On the ground the four family members had come to a halt at the end of the runway. Bertus stood like a general on the back of the pickup with his pipe clasped between his teeth. "She is a beauty," he said to those around him. Annie had her camera in her hand, and said to Sienie, "This is a historic moment for us. I am sure that Yan and Manie would like to see this on film."

Just as the airplane landed, all hell broke loose.

The aircraft touched down, as it should. Everything went as planned and for the first few hundred yards the airplane stayed on its back wheels with the nose still in the air. As soon as the nose came down, everything went horribly wrong. The nose gear gave way and then disappeared. It gave way underneath us, and the next minute we ploughed deep furrows into the runway with the nose of the aircraft.

Inside the aircraft, the sound was deafening. There was nothing that Delville could do. There was no time for fear but a sick feeling gripped my heart.

On the ground the four family members watched in horror as this drama unfolded before them. Dust folded around the airplane like a blanket and blurred their vision. The noise, even where they were standing was awful.

"Get out, get out!" Delville barked the command as soon as the aircraft came to a halt, and in a moment Bernie had the door open. He did not wait for anyone. Adrie followed and everyone scattered as far as they could from the Airplane. Delville was the last to stumble out of the damaged aircraft.

"My boetie," Sienie grabbed me around the neck and cried. Adrie was in a state of shock. Manie was white in his face and was standing with his hands over his head.

I was shocked to silence like everyone else. "What happened Delville?" I broke the silence and looked over to the Pilot standing there in his neatly dressed white uniform.

"Someone wants you guys dead for sure." He paused for a few seconds, and then said: "Look, I have flown thousands of hours in my life. I have seen strange things, but I have never seen anything like this."

The once proud Aero Commander was sitting in an awkward position. The nose was pointing into the ground and the one side of the wing was sitting higher than the other. She did not look good.

"We should have been dead now," Delville said. "The Airplane should have tumbled over the nose, and fallen on its back. If that happened, it would have caught on fire," he explained.

Suddenly my mind started working again. I am no quitter, but I wanted out of this situation. I did not belong here. I did not plan for this. Nothing about this was right and all I needed now, was a door to walk through, out of this mess.

I decided right there. "One more shipment. That's all, and I am leaving this mess. Manie can have it."

These events have been etched into my brain forever. Your life becomes a horror movie. The things you have always seen in Hollywood have become a reality. The nightmares in your past have become the resurrected Dracula's and

he is here to suck blood.   More than you are
prepared to give...

IMPOSSIBLE COINCIDENCE

The entire morning was spent discussing the events of the last two days. While we all took turns to color in the events of that morning, everyone sat still and in total awe when another would talk. As soon as that person was done, someone else would jump in.

At times we would laugh when we remembered something funny. It was not funny at the time, but looking back now, we could see the humor, and laugh about it.

We laughed at Adrie who is normally such a lady, and how attached she became to that filthy plastic bag.

Adrie then filled us in about Bernie who also became sick in the airplane, but had to use the arm of his weather jacket.

We laughed at the way everyone said: "Amen," after I prayed, and so the discussion continued.

"My boetie," Sienie said in her familiar tone. "I told you that I don't trust any of these people, and to be quite honest with you, I don't think we have seen the end of the problems yet. The fat lady hasn't sung yet." Around the table, everyone nodded their heads in agreement.

"This is so frustrating, because we cannot go to the authorities, as we have nothing to present as evidence," Annie said.

Finally, Bernie got a word in as well. "All I want to know is this; can someone tell me how am I

129

getting back home?" A tease went up around the table, and everyone cracked up with laughter as Annie pointed her finger upwards and said: "E.T. h-o-m-e."

The neighboring farmer came over later in the day to tell us that the phone line is back in working order. Delville left with Manie to go and call a Charter Company in Johannesburg to send an aircraft to fetch some of us.

Bernie called his work and informed them that he would be a day late.

Emotions settled down, the two ladies took Manie and me to the egg-room and showed us how fast the eggs were progressing in the incubator.

I took the time on the farm to catch up with some of the office work that needed to be done. I was teaching Annie on Database programs for the computer, and Sienie was looking over my shoulder to learn also.

It was hot. The Botswana temperature can easily reach one hundred and fifty. Today was no exception. The summer crickets were buzzing to a droning choir. Outside in the yard, Bertus had a cement tank which they were using as a pool, and the rest of the men were there enjoying a few minutes of cool relaxation.

"The Government is requiring so many records on these birds Yan, we can hardly keep up with all their requirements," Annie said.

For a few hours we labored on this task. The room was filled with so much smoke. Both

Sienie and Annie are heavy smokers[7] and when we get busy like this in the office, they will smoke one cigarette after another. I didn't feel free to tell them not to smoke, because after all, this was their office and their home. I was merely their guest. As soon as I felt I could not handle anymore of it, I would excuse myself and go for a breather outside.

"Next week, Rock will join us here on the farm," I informed the two ladies. "Do you think that you will be able to put him up in your house Annie?"

All of us loved Rock so much. He is the company accountant, and a life long friend of mine. We have come a long way together since the Rhodesian war, where we fought together in the same force.

"For sure." Annie responded with ease and let me know that Rock was like a brother to all of them.

In all my life, I have never seen anyone more committed to a friend than the way Rock was. He would stick with me through thick and thin.

At present, he was in the United States, keeping things straight, but we notified him to join us the following week, because of the bookwork nightmare that the ladies were facing.

Finally, Johanna the housemaid, called us to the fire outside. "Everything is ready Mrs. Annie," This humble and hard working woman was

---

[7]Both of them have since totally surrendered their lives to Christ and are no longer smoking.

standing in the door with a dishcloth in her hands. Her white apron was always spotless and her face was never without a genuine smile. She was like a mother to all of us in the house, and everyone respected her highly.

The entire afternoon my stomach complained of hunger, and when we stepped outside, the familiar scene of a table filled with food met our smiling approval. The fire was a regular thing in the evenings and this was a time for stories, family dancing and singing. It was as common as drinking coffee for all of us. Tonight was going to be no exception. All the events of the past two days would have to be repeated again and everyone was going to find something to add to the story.

For a short time our sorrows and cares were gone. The African night swallowed it all up.

Music filled the air; the bright flames of the large African fire filled the night, until finally the first person got up and excused himself and thereafter, everyone made their way to bed.

The fire was left to burn out and for several hours the hot coals would simmer.

Early in the morning the silly hysterical laughing sounds of the hyenas would be heard snooping around and later the foxy little Jackals would join them to eat the leftovers.

This was Africa, and we all loved it!

WRONG TIMING

The brand new Cessna Airplane landed on time the next morning. A proud little man, dressed in the familiar white uniform of a Pilot with pallets on his shoulders and black trousers, stepped out onto the steps of the Aircraft.

He brought with him a mechanic and another Company Pilot who would get the Aero Commander ready enough to fly back to Johannesburg for repairs.

They were going to get the front undercarriage temporarily working enough to take off.

Delville explained to us the previous night that the Pilot will pull the nose of the aircraft up immediately at take off, and pick up speed running only on the back wheels. They would also land the aircraft in the same way.

Everyone was around the Cessna when it landed. Sounds of laughter were heard and Bernie was standing around the new pilot, talking about the safety of that aircraft.

Manie, his wife Hanlie, Bernie and Adrie would fly back with the Pilot in the brand new Cessna airplane. She was a beauty. Only a single engine, but in top condition.

Bernie assured the nervous Adrie that this aircraft was safe and that he was satisfied that the pilot had enough experience.

Manie was going to Johannesburg to arrange for an airplane we could charter for the next batch of eggs.

He also had to make final arrangements with the farmer in South Africa for the large batch that would now come to our newly leased facility in Ellisras.

After all these arrangements he would go back to the United States where he was in charge of the quarantine station. His presence was needed there soon, as a batch of eggs was about to hatch.

I could not help but notice Delville standing off in the distance, talking with the Pilot of the newly chartered airplane. He was talking about us because I could see how he was throwing his head in our direction. He was obviously talking about the threats on our lives and warning the new Pilot.

The next minute, pandemonium broke out all around us. Army personnel broke out from the surrounding bushes.

Military vehicles, recklessly ran over fences, and several army helicopters arrived on the scene, circling above us, with soldiers standing behind their M60 machine guns in the open door of the choppers, pointing them down at us.

Consternation broke out all around. The women started screaming, and Annie's grandchildren cried hysterically as they nervously tried to hide behind her skirts.

The temperamental ostriches ran wildly into fences, some breaking their legs, some breaking their necks and several other remarkable injuries.

Soldiers jumped off the back of the vehicles and ran towards us, with their Ak47 rifles pointed menacingly at us.

Adrie broke into a run, and I grabbed her just in time as she tried to race past me.

"Don't be stupid," I yelled at her. "These men will kill you when you run."

I have dealt with situations like these during the war, and I knew that it would not take much for these power crazed soldiers to pull their triggers, and once they started they would not stop until everyone was dead.

Soldiers came and stood behind each of us, pointing their loaded guns at our backs, with their fingers dangerously tight around the triggers.

Anger got a hold of me, and I turned to face the soldier behind me.

"I demand to know what is going on here right now," I said in a domineering manner.

The next minute, this arrogant soldier pushed the barrel of his machine gun into my mouth, bruising my lips as the barrel was forced a few inches in, almost breaking my front teeth.

For the first time in my life, I actually looked down the barrel of a gun. I faced death once again as I looked at the white knuckle of this nervous soldier with his finger on the trigger.

The sober warning from Manie telling me to calm down brought me back to my senses.

Finally, the commander of this terrorist mob walked up to me and asked if I was in charge of this farm.

I signaled to him with my eyes that the machine gun barrel was still in my mouth and, with the motion of his hand; the barrel was slowly taken out.

My eyes followed the man with the gun, and for the first time in many years, I felt like taking someone on in hand combat.

I wanted to cause the man harm. My human nature was rebelling against this injustice, but then the sharp bark of this commander brought me back to reality.

"I asked you a question!" The man stood menacingly in front of me, with his hand over his holster.

"Yes, I am, and what is it to you! Who are you and what right have you to invade our privacy the way you are?"

"I am asking the questions and you only give the answers." The man stood in front of me, and tried to intimidate me with the white of his eyes.

I did not budge, but at the same time, I knew that I should not push the matter.

"Well, tell me then, why are you here and what is it that you want?" I asked him, with my voice shaking with the emotions of anger.

A jeep stopped next to me, and I was told to step onto the back of the vehicle. The commander and two other soldiers stepped onto the back with me, and the nervous soldier kept his rifle pointing at my belly as we rode over the rough road on the way back to the farm yard.

Sienie, Annie, and the rest followed us in our own vehicles, with a convoy of soldiers following behind them.

As we drove into the yard, I was amazed at how many soldiers were there already. The place looked like a war zone, and our workers were rounded up and standing underneath the big tree in the yard.

Fear was very visible on their faces, and as I stepped down from the Jeep, I spoke to them in a reassuring way. "Don't be afraid, we will get this thing under control in just a little while."

Sienie and Annie had gotten their composure back also. Their normal fearless attitude was back, and Annie was barking out instructions to her workers.

Sienie immediately took position at her egg room like a guard and even after she was told to step aside, she refused.

"If you go in here, there are procedures you will have to follow," she said, pointing her finger at the soldier. She tried to explain in vain about the dangers of contamination etc, but ruthlessly the man pushed her aside and she stumbled on her feet as several of the men followed the leader into the egg room.

"Do not let them in there by themselves Sienie," I shouted from where they held me at bay with the rifle still pointed to my chest.

Sienie walked into the egg-room behind them and watched the men handle the sensitive, and expensive eggs with their bare hands.

One of the soldiers pulled a handkerchief from his pocket to wipe a nervous sweat from his brow, when a marker pen fell from his pocket.

Sienie's eyes picked up on the object immediately, and it seemed as if no one else saw this happen.

She immediately positioned her foot over the pen, and stayed there even though the soldier commanded her to step aside.

"Sir, as long as you remain in this egg-room, I am instructed by my employer to remain here with you. I will not interfere with what you are doing, but it is my right to stay and make my observations. We do not trust you, and that is the end of the matter."

The surprised look on the soldiers face told Sienie that she had won the moment.

It was obvious to her that they were up to something but she could not tell what it was.

Finally, as they left the egg-room Sienie moved her foot, and picked up the marking pen, taking care to only handle it with her fingertips around the very top, so that any fingerprints may remain intact.   It turned out later to be an infrared pen![8]

"Now what would they need an infrared pen for?" She asked herself as she stuck it into the pocket of her dress.

An hour later, the vehicles started up, and suddenly peace returned to the farm as these clumsy soldiers made their way from our property.

"Now what was that all about?" I asked those around me nervously, not expecting an answer.

I still felt the rush of anger inside of me, and also knew that we were very close to meeting our Maker.

"My boetie," Sienie said to all of us.   "I believe that they were up to something in the egg-room but my presence foiled their plans."

She pulled the pen carefully from her dress pocket, handling only the tip with her fingertips, and showed it to us.   "Look, it is a Magic Marking pen according to the label, and it is infrared.

What is infrared?" She asked as she presented the pen to Manie's outstretched hand.

"It means, it is a pen that leaves a mark that cannot be seen with the naked eye," Manie said in a melancholy way.

---

[8] These infrared markers would come into play later on in the story.

"Just don't touch the pen Manie," Sienie said as she handed the pen to Manie. "This could become very important evidence in time to come."

None of us had any idea how accurate her intuition was.

****

Manie and the rest of the crew, boarded the airplane, and we stood there on the fairway, watching until the aircraft cut through a thin selection of clouds and disappeared from sight.

Delville and the other two men got started on our airplane, and by the end of the afternoon, we watched as the new Pilot raced the engine to top revolutions, and as soon as he released the break, lifted the nose of the wounded bird, and picked up speed running only on the two rear wheels. The take-off went without any problems, and they too, disappeared through the clouds.

Manie was sitting next to the Pilot of the Cessna when all of a sudden; a fire broke out underneath the dashboard of the airplane. Bernie told me afterwards, that he decided there and then that he would never again fly in another small aircraft. The Pilot grabbed the extinguisher and put the small fire out. Somehow a short broke out inexplicably and everyone was left very nervous.

Near Johannesburg, the Pilot put the airplane down safely at the Wonderboom Airport, but when they got to the customs desk, was told to fly

140

to Jan Smuts Airport, as they were not ready to check the passengers in at that location for the day.

The nervous Pilot told Manie he found this very strange. He said that he had never encountered that kind of response from them. A man was standing around the Cessna as they walked back to it, and when they came close, he turned and walked over to another aircraft, that was parked next to the Cessna.

A couple of hundred feet into the air, things suddenly went wrong. The engine stopped and pandemonium broke loose. The Aircraft went down fast! The Pilot was frantically trying to get the motor started again but without any success.

Underneath them there was no place to land. They were over a heavily populated housing area.

The Pilot finally gave up trying to start the engine and started concentrating on putting the aircraft down.

"Check your safety belts and prepare for a hard landing," he shouted out nervously. Adrie could not believe her eyes. "This was not happening. This is just a nightmare and I will wake up in a few seconds," she said to herself, but then she felt the arm of her husband around her, and he shouted for her to hold on for dear life.

Adrie came back to reality. She was awake and she knew it now. For the third time in three days, she was involved in an emergency landing, and this time it did not look good at all.

Everyone in the aircraft started saying their final prayers. Their lives started shooting past them like a flash. At that point nothing else mattered as much as eternity.

The ground was approaching fast now. The pilot was trying his best to keep the airplane steady but the wings were flopping up and down from side to side.

Manie could not believe his eyes. As they were coming in for the landing in one of the local streets, a man in a Mercedes Benz was looking back over his shoulder at the approaching airplane, and instead of coming to a dead stop, it seemed as if he wanted to race the aircraft to the end of the road.

"What is that guy trying to do?" Manie asked out aloud, but did not really expect an answer.

The nervous, young pilot was busy with his own problems, but still he answered: "Well, I am going to have to land on top of him. There is nothing else I can do."

At the last minute the Mercedes Benz driver realized what was going on and swerved his car out of the road and into a nearby drive way.

The next few minutes are ineradicably tattooed into every one's mind. The aircraft took a few hops, and then seemingly glued the wheels to the pavement, but just as everyone started to relax, the right wing connected with a telephone pole and cut the wing off on the one side.

Fuel went spurting out all over the street. The noise was almost unbearable! The aircraft spun around a few times. Inside the airplane, everyone expected to die at that moment.

It seemed as if they were on a roller coaster from hell. Madness was in the place of pleasure and no one was at the control of this fearful ride.

All of a sudden everything was over. The Pilot yelled out at the top of his lungs. "Out! Out, quickly, she is going to catch on fire."

For the second time in two days, Bernie found himself bursting towards the door. This time, he pushed Adrie out first, and then as she fell to the ground, he jumped like a tiger to the street right behind her and scooped his crying wife up in his arms with almost super human strength.

Her arms were folded around his neck and she cried hysterically. The tension inside this frail little lady was just too much.

Without even noticing her weight, Bernie ran like a young roe with his wife in his arms away from the scene. Madness had almost become part of him, and only when a sympathetic bystander stopped him and helped him to lower his wife to the ground did he come back to his normal senses.

Manie, Hanlie and the young pilot were not far behind them, and when their feet hit the ground they started running. Any moment the Aircraft could catch on fire and the explosion would throw them into the air.

As they finally came to a halt they realized that nothing like that had happened. Both of them were out of breath, and the pilot started yelling at people to get away from the airplane. Danger was still all around. A slight spark would ignite the scene like a bomb. Fuel was still streaming out from what was left behind of the one wing.

"Sweet Jesus," the Pilot finally said with a sigh of relief, as he lifted his head towards the heavens. The words uttered were not meant to be profanity, but a sigh from the lips of a man who realized that the fact that they all escaped with their lives, were nothing short of a genuine miracle from God.

Bernie was sitting on the sidewalk with Adrie. He was talking unendingly and relief was written all over his face.

Adrie had settled down and as Manie walked up to them Bernie muttered: "To think that Adrie and I were sitting peacefully in our home on a normal Saturday afternoon when you and Yan walked into our house. Since then, nothing has been normal at all. I mean we have been in three emergency landings in two days. Nobody is going to believe me."

The man kept on talking until Manie finally broke the tension with his spontaneous laughter and said "Yeah, but think about it this way, you came thru alive every time, and you actually live to tell this story."

Bernie snorted back at Manie and the people around him laughed at the lighthearted discussion going on between two of the victims.

Someone in the crowd volunteered to take the three of them to their waiting car at Jan Smuts Airport, and without waiting for the police to arrive; they got into the car.

Just before they drove off the young pilot came and knocked on the window and protested. "This is an accident scene and you are not to leave.

Manie calmly looked at the stressed out young man and said: "We did not make the accident, and you have our name and address. Tell the police to contact us if they need any more information. We are going home now."

With that answer hanging in the air, he tapped the friendly man next to him on the shoulder, and said: "Let's go sir."

With the Pilot swinging his hands in disgust, Manie and the rest of them disappeared around the corner.

READY, STEADY, GO!

The rains kept on coming down for days without end until little streams turned into torrents.

It does not take much for the lowveld in that part of the country to come alive. Years of drought had brought the place to the brink of destruction, but now after weeks of interminable rain, the place was turning into the paradise that it actually is.

The trees appeared to be standing proudly erect and were pushing branches forward that were now filled with new leaves.

The Tuli-Block, where our farm was situated, was no exception, and the place came alive. Everything blossomed and even the workers on the farm, seemed to receive new energy.

The long rains, turned the already bad roads into a nightmare and only people with strong, four wheel-drive vehicles could make it out on these unpaved, poorly developed roads. Bridges were washed away and it seemed the Botswana Government was going to take forever to get to the task of repairing them.

Flowers appeared out of nowhere and suddenly Africa looked pretty again. Within weeks the thin, worn out game developed a shine on their skin, which they did not have a few weeks before. The tiredness in them disappeared and now they were so alert that you could hardly notice them before they would run wildly into the thick dense brush. The Tambotie-grass reached up and before long, the stems would reach their normal six to seven feet tall.

Every thing was back to normal. Bontshe, our farm, was no exception. The Ostriches seemed to enjoy the rain also and even though these birds would stand over eight feet tall, they now acted like any other bird. They took baths in the puddles of rain, they ran, they engaged in fake fights with one another. They would spin and dance, wings opening as if they could fly, and the proud males would bellow out the sounds of their territorial proclamations.

Bontshe was doing wonderfully good. It was time for another shipment and this one would go to our own quarantine station in Los Angeles. We were almost at the point of supplying all the eggs to our investor friends, and thereafter things would return to normal for us.

All I wanted to see was that my friends in the USA would not lose out, and that they would make the kind of profits that I knew were possible. Then, I would be released from this horrible experience and get back to the work of the Ministry which I loved so much.

I felt like David in the camp of the Philistines when he was running from King Saul.

Rock, my life long friend, arrived on the farm. He was like a breath of fresh air to me. For many years we used to sing together. We made records together, and it was therefore no strange occurrence to me when he stopped into the yard, that the first thing that came out of his car was his guitar. He lifted it high up in the air and with me still standing in the distance, we laughed like two young teenagers.

I felt good when my friend threw his arms around me for a friendly hug. I knew he meant it! Some people hug you and you don't feel safe, but not Rock. He was the most sincere person I had ever met. Here was a man, who even though he could not quit smoking, was possibly one of the most sincere Christians I had ever met.

He was solid as a Rock, and I smiled to myself as we walked over to the chairs outside, to sit down for a chat. Someone gave him the correct name. Rock!

My two sisters came and joined us, and excitedly for several hours, we told Rock about the recent events. His head would turn from one person to another as we would each take a turn to fill him in. Then when one person seemed to forget the slightest detail, someone else would take up the rest of the story and complete it. Like Annie used to say to us, "Look, if you're going to tell the story, tell it in such a way that the other person can see it happen."

We talked until the late hour of the night. Then later that evening, Rock and I sang around the fire. Some of the workers came and sat around the fire also, listening to the two white men sing. I heard some of them say in their typical African manner: "Hau, Henna Mnandi."[9]

The day blinked its eye, and finally, we had to call an end to it. Tomorrow, we will accept a new challenge. This day is over, and finally the only sounds that could be heard from Bontshe in the Tuli Block, were the night crickets, and the

---

[9] "Wow, this is nice"

call of a lonely Jackal that was waiting his turn around the remains of our fire.

CHAPTER 4

PLANNED FAILURE

THE BEGINNING OF THE END

"Everything has been set up Yan. The bacon is on the way to the oven and an airplane will be on the farm Friday morning to pick up the next shipment of eggs."

I knew what Manie was talking about. We had agreed to be very careful on the phone because of the bugs someone had placed on the lines. Before he left we decided to use certain code words. For our Ellisras venture in the Northern Transvaal, we would refer to the Incubators as "the oven", and the eggs will be the "bacon."

We were going to accept Piet's advise to take no chances at all, and we moved with double caution on everything we did.

Manie explained to me that he was flying back to the States the following morning. Even though I understood the reason why he had to leave, I still envied him greatly.

"We are going to do this shipment so good that we will have the State Veterinarian impressed," Annie told us. No one believed her as they smiled, but at least it caused a moment of humor. Every one of us knew and understood that when the State Veterinarian arrived on the farm, he was merely a messenger from the President and was instructed to make things as hard as possible for us.

Sienie, who was in charge of the eggs in the coolers, had taken care to wash them extra clean.

Manie discovered a safe solvent, which took all the dirt out of the pores of the eggs as well as any other substance.

A Veterinarian in Los Angeles recommended this method to us, as he explained that a whole lot of hatching problems could be avoided before incubation even started.

"The egg is a live object and as soon as it reaches the correct temperature incubation starts immediately thereafter. The Embryo breathes through the pores of the egg," he explained to Manie. "We have to minimize infection from the outset,"

As usual, Sienie took her job very seriously and scrubbed each egg with a hard brush in this soapy solvent.

When she opened the cooler door for me to admire her handiwork, I could not help but to be genuinely impressed. The fourteen hundred eggs were ready to be shipped. They were not only ready, but they were shining like pearls freshly brought out of the water.

"Just as you ordered them, my boetie." She presented her work to me, by taking a slight bow and her hand making a sweeping motion from her body into the cooler.

All the eggs were numbered from the first to the last one, as required by the State Veterinarian.

Each egg can be traced back to a particular Ostrich pen, and subsequently also to a particular bird.

The system we had in place would tell us how productive each bird was and even the fertility rate of each bird's eggs.

Rock and Annie were heavily involved with the paper trail, and now that Rock was here I knew that it would take only a short while and things will be flowing as they should as far as the administration goes.

"Well Sienie," I said after looking at the eggs, "In two days, the next airplane will be here to pick up this shipment."

We went for a stroll up to the little chick-pens and talked. "I don't know why, my boetie," Sienie said after a short silence. "I feel sick inside my stomach. I am not sick, but I don't know what is going on. Something is happening behind the scenes that we are unaware of. Are you keeping something away from us?"

I assured her that I had no hidden agenda. The folks on the farm knew about our Ellisras venture and there was nothing that Manie and I was not telling them.

"Are you doing all right financially Yan?"

I assured her that everything was going well. The sales in the United States were a little slower than usual, but we were not concerned about it. Things were normal, but I had the same nagging gut feeling. I didn't tell her this, because I did not want to alarm anyone.

Two days later the airplane that Manie ordered, landed on time. She was big and all the seats had been taken out.

The pilot was friendly and I told him about our unfortunate experience over the past few days.

"Don't you worry," he told me without smiling. "Delville told me about all those problems, and I made double sure about my safety and the safety of my aircraft. "

He assured me that unless a time bomb had been planted there was no chance of anything going wrong, as he flew straight to the farm without any problems.

"As long as we don't allow any strangers near our airplane, we will be in good shape," the man explained seriously.

The State Veterinarian sent another person in his place to check the shipment. This Veterinarian notified us that he would only check the eggs but he had no authority to sign the export papers. He explained that the eggs would still have to go via Gaberone where the State Veterinarian would sign the papers.

We needed no discernment to understand that something was going on which we did not know about. My stomach gave several disturbing turns and although I did not know what was going on, my sixth sense told me that trouble was lurking up ahead.

I abandoned the fear inside, as I knew that everything was legal and as long as the Veterinarian passed the packing of the shipment, no other problems would occur.

Bertus and Barry were supervising the loading of the eggs themselves and the boxes were packed carefully.

The pilot took me by the arm and walked to the side where we were out of hearing. "I don't know what is going on Mr. Venter, but someone at the airport in Johannesburg, told me that you were heading for some real trouble."

I felt my stomach tighten and this time it seemed as if my skin was crawling. I looked at the man with shock.

"What kind of trouble?" He shrugged his head and told me that was all he heard. "I am just your Pilot, but I do know that something is going on for sure. Do you have all your paperwork in order?" he asked me. I assured him that there was no way that we would take any chances with such an expensive shipment.

The shipment was going to be done with two trips. I would accompany the first one, and while I was getting the eggs into the main building he would make a run for the second batch.

The flight to Gaborone took less than an hour. Everything went smoothly and we were cleared for landing immediately.

From then on everything was outlandish. We could not find anyone to help us offload the boxes of eggs, and the pilot and I had to do this laborious task on our own.

The heat of the sun was excruciatingly hot. I loaded the boxes onto a trolley, and as the pilot departed for the next batch, I struggled on my own to get the eggs into a shady spot. I found it strange that no one on the airport would offer any assistance to get the eggs out of the hot sun into a cooler place.

"Was I imagining it, or was there a sense of animosity in everyone I was trying to talk to?" I mumbled these questions to myself, but then assured myself, that I had become totally paranoid. "You are expecting an enemy behind every person's shadow Yan, and you should stop this right now." My self-rebuke did not work and the feeling in my heart got stronger and stronger.

I could not leave the eggs where they were, so I decided to go into the main building and get a hold of a manager of sorts to complain to.

It was not uncommon to find an unfriendly atmosphere among African people working for the government. Now, it was even worst. Not one person wanted to talk to me. I felt so helpless and I was frantically trying to get someone to understand that the eggs cannot stay in that excruciating heat outside, but no one was willing to listen to me. Frustration and fear now gripped my heart with a fresh intensity.

Suddenly my heart almost came to a standstill. The same two men from before walked straight by me. This time, totally ignoring me.

I was totally overwhelmed. "What is going on here?" They walked out through the security with not one person stopping them. I went and stood by the window looking at them as they were walking away from me. "They are certainly up to something," I said to myself as I kept an eye on them.

To my surprise they walked straight to our batch of eggs, and all of a sudden several local people were there to assist them. My surprise got even bigger when they started to load our eggs onto a truck that drove up for the task.

I tried to get outside, but security blocked me from leaving the building "without a permit."

"What permit?" I asked the security man in bewilderment. "There are two thieves out there, stealing my shipment of eggs."

I felt my head spinning. "What is going on here?" I kept asking myself, but no answers would come to me.

All of a sudden two other sinister looking men appeared next to me. They introduced themselves to me as "Special task force to the President" or something to that nature.

I realized that if I ever looked into the face of two real hoodlums, it was these two men. Their expressions reminded me of the mafia type which you see in the movies when they were sent by the crime boss to collect his bounty from innocent businessmen.

My fear was turned into anger when I said in an obnoxious manner, "Sir, if you are working for the President then I ask you to accompany me outside to where those men are illegally loading up our shipment of eggs onto that truck.

It was obvious to me at that moment that those two hoodlums outside and these two mafia swindlers, were working on the same team.

Somehow my mind just did not want to accept the facts as they appeared. "How can those two men be involved with the President of Botswana? They were following me as early as the Namibian days, and then Swaziland" None of these things made any sense, but then my mind came to a halt, when these two men next to me insisted that I walk to a little room with them. They informed me that they have reason to believe that I am involved in arms smuggling.

"Arms smuggling?" I was so shocked that I jumped up and allowed my chair to fall over backwards. "Arms smuggling!" I was never more speechless and angry than at that moment. I did not know whether I should laugh or cry at this ludicrous indictment.

"Listen, you must have the wrong person in mind. There is just no way that you will be able to pin this one on me," I objected in vain.

I finally realized that the less I said, the better it would be. I looked at one of the men. "Sir, I am an American Citizen, and I demand that my rights as a citizen be honored. It is my right to make a phone call and to contact an attorney."

The two men laughed in an ugly way. Their laughter told me that I was in real danger. A bigger danger than I had faced before, and that included the Aero Commander experience earlier on.

I tried to stay calm. I have learned from experiences in the past, that you don't think clear when you are upset.

I took a deep breath, and allowed my mind a few moments to come back to normal. My mouth was so dry right now, if only I could get some water, but somehow I just knew that nothing I would ask them would be given to me.

My mind went out to the pilot and I was wondering what was happening to him. I was thinking about my people on the farm, and how Annie would handle this situation as sick as she was.

My mind just did not want to stand still. One question after another raced through it until it felt that I was going to go crazy.

The two men left me alone in the little room for what seemed an eternity, and when they finally returned, I was told to follow them.

"No sir," I said, with determination in my voice. "I am not going anywhere with you. I don't know you, I need to see some identification and if you are arresting me, I want to hear you read me my rights, and you need to tell me what you are arresting me for."

The older one of the two men grabbed me on the arm. His grip was so tight, that his nails bit into the soft part of my upper arm.

He hissed the words out when he spoke: "You can either walk out here with us, or we can have you carried out on a stretcher. Either way you are coming with us." His eyes reminded me of a snake, and his teeth were yellow. His breath

158

smelled like something had died in there. These were two dangerous men. They had the President on their side, and I knew that my life was in real danger.

"Furthermore," he continued, "I would not put Annie and Sienie's lives at stake if I was you."

This caught me off guard, and he noticed my surprise. "Aha, you did not know that I knew about them too, did you?" He laughed at me, and I looked into his ugly mouth. I felt so tempted to put my fist into his face.

Many such thoughts went through my mind, but for the sake of my sisters on the farm, I obliged the two men, and walked out with them.

They took me out to a waiting aircraft and when I stepped inside, the two hoodlums from before were in there waiting.

"You thought you were funny when you set those bees on us," one of the men spoke to me.

This time it was my turn to laugh, and I did it in an ugly way. I let the stress out when I laughed. He pulled his hand back to hit me, but one of the President's hoodlums stopped him and said: "No, no. He is not yours. He belongs to us." The stubborn streak in me took over and I continued to mock him now.

No one told me where we were going, but my senses picked up on a northern direction, and I guessed that we were heading for Bontshe, our farm in the Tuli Block.

My suspicions were confirmed when all of a sudden; ol' satan's kopje appeared over in the distance.

Down underneath I noticed that things were not normal. As we circled the airstrip to land, I noticed many military vehicles on our farm.

The once tranquil scene was not turned into what seemed to be a military zone.

As soon as we landed, a military jeep was next to the airplane to transport us to the farmhouse.

The soldiers were all armed to the teeth. The place looked like a war zone. The farmyard was no exception and the place was crawling with soldiers.

No one was doing anything. They were obviously waiting on us. As soon as we arrived, the soldiers went to work with the two hoodlums walking around as they pleased. They turned the place upside down. Drawers were pulled out of the closet and mattresses were turned upside down. They looked underneath the loose rugs on the floor and every nook and corner was searched. We did not know what they were searching for, but kept out of their way as much as possible.

Our workers were sitting underneath a tree crying. Men and women were crying, and Johannes was looking at me with an expression of sorrow. "We had become such good friends," I thought to myself as I winked at him and forced a smile.

Annie was doing well, but she was white in the face. She was fighting mad. "Don't worry about this Yan," she said. "As soon as I can get to a phone, I am calling the American Consulate. These wicked people are going to have to explain to someone about this." Annie was talking to me in Afrikaans. None of the men with me could understand what she was saying, and told her to speak in English or to "shut-up." She ignored him and talked to me some more, only to frustrate the man.

Sienie was emotional. Like Annie, she was mad, but she was like a mother all around me. "My boetie, have they been treating you all right?" She was talking through the tears, and I felt so sorry for the two of them. In fact, I felt so sorry for all our workers. This must be a terrible blow for all of them to see me being held captive this way.

I forced a smile and winked at Sienie and Annie, trying to console them as much as I could.

In the Afrikaans language, I instructed them in short sentences, what they should do, and who to contact. The man with me was so frustrated because he could not understand a word we were saying and he could not get us to work with him to keep our discussions in English.

Suddenly the back door opened and one of the two hoodlums came out together with one of the President's Security men. They had discovered ten rounds of live ammunition, which Bertus kept in his closet. This ammunition was left over after satan bit the dust. The rifle was handed back to the neighbor but the ammunition was kept for use next time.

The older man with the ugly, yellow teeth came and stood over me while I was sipping on a cup of hot tea.

"So, we have the proof we need to arrest you on. We know that you are an International Arms

Smuggler and this is all the evidence we need."
He lifted the bullets up like a trophy and while
others were still sweeping through the place, I
was told to get back on the Jeep.

Sienie and Annie with their husbands were
standing helpless as I climbed back onto the
jeep.

All our computers and office files were taken.
Anything that appeared to be of any value was
loaded into a big truck, and we had absolutely no
say in the matter.

The atmosphere was bad. It was the worst day
of my life. I had never felt like this before. It
felt as if the blood had drained from my face.

As the airplane took off from the airstrip, heading
back to Gaborone, I realized that this wrench in
my hand just got unbearable. "God, please
help me", I cried. My whole world had just
collapsed into a mud puddle.

MARKS ON THE EGGS.

The ride in the airplane back to Gaborone was one of the worst days in my life. For the first time in many years I felt real hatred.

The last time I felt this way, was when I was in the Rhodesian war, and our unit was sweeping an area in search of some real hardcore terrorists. These terrorists were developed behind the iron curtain, and they were well-trained killers.

At the time when I was drafted into the war, I did not know if I would be able to carry a weapon against another human. I was pastor of a small church and to me this would be the total opposite from trying to save people's lives.

This unsure feeling left me when I walked into a small mission church where two of the missionary ladies were killed. They were violently crucified upside down on the doorframe of the church. They were nailed through the feet with six-inch nails. We found them hanging there naked and their private parts cut out.

That day I hated the evil in the men who had done such a wicked thing. I hated not the men, but oh, I hated the evil and I knew I could track those men down and bring them to justice, one way or another!

Now, as I was sitting there, looking at the hoodlums in front of me, I felt hatred. I am embarrassed to admit to this, but I did. This was so unfair. Everything was so illegal and a dream went up in smoke.

When I watched them walk around freely in and out of Annie's house, and kicking things around, I just knew that they somehow were linked with the airplane disasters, the Swaziland affair and all the other miseries that we were not even aware of at the time.

All my life I disliked bullies. I have a low tolerance in my spirit for someone that likes to take advantage over someone weaker than them. These four hoodlums were the epitome of bullies. I disliked them.

They were laughing and having a good time drinking ice-cold sodas in front of me, but no one offered any to me. I was thinking to myself however, that even if they were to offer I would not accept.

I will never forget the look in my family's eyes or even that of our workers as these so-called lawmen arrested me on the charges of arms smuggling. They knew that there was no way they could make these charges stick in a court of law.

The United States was just then building an airbase in Gaborone and I said to myself that I had to just stay alive until I could appear in court. The government could not afford an international incident and as a USA citizen I would have to get a fair trail.

Half way through the flight to Gaborone the men leaned forward into a circle and in a whisper had a meeting for several minutes. I knew they were talking about me because every now and again one of them would look over their shoulder to me. I could not hear what they were saying because of the noise of the engine.

After the meeting, one of them took out a cell phone and made a call to somewhere. He stayed on line for several minutes. After the call was made they huddled together once more while the telephone caller informed the others of the conversation. Every one was obviously in agreement because they all shook their heads and the meeting was over.

I turned my head and looked out of the window. I have decided not to open my mouth other than to give them my name and address. Nothing more will be said, until I have spoken to an attorney.

The rest of the way to Gaborone, I spent thinking: "Where in the world am I going to find anyone in Botswana, ready to defend me." I realized that such a person should be willing to stand up against the President of Botswana! "Who will be willing to do that though?"

The perfect landing on the Gaborone airport told me that this pilot was good. He was not part of the kangaroo unit. The aircraft was obviously chartered by these men and as I stepped out of the aircraft, I thought I noticed a reassuring smile in his eyes.

My suspicions were confirmed as I made my way out of the airplane. All the others were already outside and standing in a circle. "They were possibly discussing their next plan of action," I said to myself.

Just as I was ready to move outside, I heard the pilot whisper a warning to me: "I would be very careful with these men if I was you sir." I looked over my shoulder to him with surprise. "You are in real danger. Don't say anything, and get yourself an attorney right away."

I wanted to ask him to contact an attorney for me, as I did not know any in Botswana, but he put his point finger over his lips, indicating for me with his eyes, not to let out that he was talking to me.

I jumped down from the airplane onto the tarmac. Calmness had come over me. I knew what I had to do now and every move from here on would be well thought out.

My hands were cuffed behind my back and I was roughly pushed towards an airplane hangar, which was a little way from the main building.

I did not resist them and walked toward the building that they indicated to me.

Thankfulness had come over me when I felt the dryness in my mouth was gone. I was no longer nervous or scared. I had cleared my head and for the first time since that morning, I was thinking straight. My eyes were missing nothing and every part of my surroundings was taken in.

The hangar door was closed, but I was pushed to go through a small door on the side. I was not a little bit surprised when I walked into the building and the entire shipment of eggs was there. All the boxes were open and it was clear that the eggs have been handled. Many of them were sticking out of the boxes, and whoever had done this, did not even take the time to hide the fact that this was so.

There were quite a few people in the hangar. I did not know any of them.

"We have reason to believe that these eggs were purchased by you in the Republic of South Africa, in the Northern Cape, and you smuggled then into Botswana, for export to the United States." It was one of the President's hoodlums who was speaking to me and I merely looked at him defiantly.

"What have you to say about this?" the man asked while standing in front of me. I was incredibly angry. They know that they cannot make the "Arms Smuggling" case stick against me, now they want to pull this trick. My lips were pulled into a thin line. I could feel myself bite down on my jaw, and I looked at him with fire in my eyes.

"We were on the farm when these eggs were loaded. We followed the truck for miles, and somewhere in the Northern Transvaal we lost track of it," the other hoodlum said to me.

Stubbornness had now gotten a hold of me. The fiery preacher from a few months ago was not here today. I was in a rage, like never before.

One of the other two hoodlums came and stood in front of me. He had a very weak chin and his eyes were sitting too close to each other. His nose looked like it had been broken once before and he had an ugly scar on the side of his neck. He stretched his fingers forward and stuck four of them into my chest saying: "Did you hear we were talking to you old man?"

I broke my silence and looked the man up close in his eyes, with my chin pushed out to him. "Why don't you untie my hands and then push 'this old man' again the way you just did!" For a moment his eyes turned to look at his companions, but then he looked back at me, and laughed his ugly laugh again.

A fat man with a round face walked up to me and introduced himself as a sergeant from the South African Police. He said his name was Koos[10].

He told me that him and "someone else" was on the farm in the Northern Cape when eggs were purchased there under our name. "We placed an infra-red dot on each of the eggs that left the farm that day," he explained.

I believed the man. I believe he was there when the eggs were purchased for our Ellisras venture in the Northern Transvaal, but they had their facts wrong.

I smiled as I remembered how well Sienie washed each egg, and even if this was true and it was not, any marks would have been dissolved by the strong solvent, which we used. Sienie even scrubbed the eggs. I did not say anything about this fact, but I merely smiled into the fat man's face and said: "Well, why don't you show me the marks then?"

"That is what we are going to do right now Mr. Venter, and with your permission we want to unpack all these eggs one by one."

With a grin on my face I told the man: "I give you no permission, but I am also not stupid sir. These eggs have already been taken out of the

---

[10] I later nicknamed him as "Fat Koos" and the name stuck to him. Even those four hoodlums would later refer to him in the same manner.

boxes. For the record kindly note that all these boxes are open."

As if he did not hear what I said, they started unpacking the eggs and placing them onto cardboard boxes on the floor. "Nothing is sterile here," I thought to myself but then again, "it does not really matter anymore. These eggs have been in the sun and in this hot aircraft hangar for too long. These eggs will be dead by now."

After the eggs were placed on the cardboard boxes, the fat policeman from South Africa walked over to his briefcase, and fetched his infrared light. He was sweating profusely. He looked uncomfortable even while he was walking. His upper thighs rubbed against each other and his khaki trousers made a whooshing kind of a noise.

I was not surprised at all when the eggs all carried markings on them. They had the whole day to work on these eggs, while I was taken to the farm. What they did not know was that the real eggs were on the farm by now in Ellisras.

What an incredible joke this was!

As I looked into the eyes of the two hoodlums I realized that this was not a joke at all though. They were looking at me with venom in the eyes.

Silence had gotten a hold of me again, and the stubborn streak was back in my spirit.

"Do you deny any of this?" the fat man asked me, while wiping the sweat from his face with a dirty handkerchief. He looked irritated and could not help but to show it.

"I need to hear you answer, sir." He said to me. I looked calmly at this man who wasn't a threat to me at all and said: "My name is Yan Gabriel Venter. I am one of the owners of the farm called Bontshe. I am a citizen of the United States of America, and I demand my right to an attorney. More than this I have nothing to say to you or to anyone else in this building." The fat man was wiping the sweat off his face again and I was wondering how it must feel for a fellow like him to be in this position where he knows that as an officer of the law he is in cahoots with hoodlums, the likes of these men.

I felt no threat from these men but several other men from Botswana were there staring angrily at me. I could not help to remember the warning of the Pilot a little while ago when he warned that my life was in danger.

The stubborn streak in me had gotten a hold of me once again and it was hard to shake it loose.

JAIL TIME

The jail cell was the dirtiest hole I have ever seen in my life. The filthy blanket with holes the size of saucers in it was not something I could use to cover myself with. The hole in the ground next to me, which was used as a toilet, was extremely dirty. The smell was almost unbearable and I knew that before long, I would have to use it.

My jailors enjoyed the moment when the two hoodlums first handed me over to them. They left me standing in a corner of the office. My eyes scanned the room quick. The room was filled with old and dirty woodwork. The one desk had the untidy remains of bread on an open piece of brown paper. A container of milk with some of it spilled over the one side of the desk was typical of every other piece of décor in the room. The floor was in desperate need of a broom, and a few flies were zooming over a dirty dishcloth on the other desk.

The little crowd huddled in another corner of the room and they obviously discussed my situation. Something was said and they laughed while everyone turned to me. The two hoodlums walked up to me and said: "Well Mr. Ostrich[11], we are going to leave you in the very capable hands of this Lieutenant and his people. He slapped me on the side of the head as he walked by me and at that moment I wished my hands

---

[11] Only the President called me by that name.

171

were not cuffed. Thoughts of wrath were crowding my mind and no sign of the teaching of Christ concerning this kind of treatment was anywhere close to my mind. I literally staggered at my own thoughts.

The only other person to have called me by that name was the President, and I could not help but to think about the coincidence.

"Come and let us see what you have in your pants Mr. Venter," the Lieutenant said as he un-expectantly slapped me between the legs with such force that I lost my breath for a while and while I was groaning with pain I heard the others laugh.

The night was young and much was laying ahead for me. I realized that the less I say or stare at them the better it is going to be for me.

Slowly I stood up straight as one of the men walked behind me and released the cuffs from my bruised arms. The hoodlum who set the cuffs made sure that he closed them as far as they would go. He only stopped when I cried out lightly with pain.

I was ordered to take off my clothes so that they could complete their body search. The two women that were there stood in front of me when I was commanded to place my hands over my head. At first I tried to resist but I noticed one of the jailors standing ready with a pipe in his hands and I decided it was not worth the trouble.

The women seemingly enjoyed the moment as they scoffed and mocked at my nakedness. I tried to show no embarrassment. I knew what their plans were. They wanted to expose weakness in me, but once again my stubborn nature was in place.

"Look all you want to," I said to the women in front of me. The man with the pipe in his hands made a threatening move and without blinking an eye, I looked at him defiantly but then decided to keep my mouth shut.

I have heard and read so many horror stories in the past of what had happened to men who fell in the hands of these ruthless African rulers.

As I was standing in front of them I thought of what would happen if these men could find out that I used to be involved in the Rhodesian war against the so called "freedom fighters."

It was our task to track down terrorists who have hit their so-called "soft targets," and to bring them to justice. Black people all over Africa hated these "Police, Anti-Terrorist Units", even though the men in our units were not all white.

These PATU units were well trained for the purpose of bringing these killers to justice and never was a stone left unturned to track them down no matter where the tracks led.

I realized that my life was in grave danger. Anything could spark off violence in these men. The man with the lead pipe was standing to my side and the pipe was hanging loosely in his grip.

At the slightest sign of trouble I had already decided that he was going to be my first target, and I would have to move fast. These Botswana men are mostly small in stature and I knew that if I moved fast enough I could be in charge of this situation in a short while but then I remembered my two sisters on the farm, and immediately the thoughts were summarily removed from my mind. "No, just stay calm and take it one step at a time," I told myself.

For the next half an hour, they played with me like a cat plays with a mouse but finally, when they got tired of their senseless games I was pushed into the direction of this small little cell and the heavy steel door clanged shut behind me. I knew that it would be useless to ask for my clothes at this time, so I just kept quiet once more and waited.

I stood against the wall around the door where the curious glances of my jailors through a small hole in the door, could not observe me.

I was not ready for the dirty blanket yet, so I remained against the wall, and allowed my mind to go back over the events that took place since that morning. It seemed as if all of this happened several days ago, but less than twelve hours had come and gone since my arrest.

The atmosphere in this small cell was dense. The air was thick with humidity and it was not long, before the onslaught of mosquitoes started.

Once these mosquitoes discovered me, they arrived back in hordes. The buzzing noise of a thick barrage of these hungry little insects caused me to grab the dirty blanket and cover myself as much as possible. The large holes in the blanket were so numerous though, that these bombers from hell would still penetrate and the moment they sat down on my skin, would sink their pin-like suckers deep into me.

"This is going to be a long night", I said to myself out loud. The smell of the dirty blanket was no longer a factor to be considered.

The door of my cell opened behind me and a thin, neatly dressed man summoned me to follow him.

With the dirty blanket wrapped around me, I followed the man into the Lieutenant's office. The man was looking at me with a smile that reminded me of the devil himself.

"You sign this paper, and we will let you go right now." The man offered a white sheet of paper to me, but without receiving it from his hand, I shook my head in total defiance.

The man cursed me, and sent me back to my cell. Before walking through the open door, another man appeared behind me and pulled the blanket from my person. His hands were placed between my shoulders and he pushed me into the dirty place.

"You need a wash, you stink," the man said and lifted a bucket from the floor. The contents were sprayed over me and I realized then, that it was not water, but a bucket full of urine.

The dirty blanket was finally thrown into the cell in front of me, and the door banged shut again. The little peephole opened up and I heard the giggling noises behind the door.

This was going to undeniably be the test of my life. I leaned forward; picked up the dirty blanket and wiped myself dry as much as possible. My eyes were burning and I realized that the mosquitoes were going to have a fun time now.

The next hour was spent making war against more and more of these little pests that were relentlessly coming after me.

The scent of the urine on my sweaty body became an unavoidable attraction to them.

Three more times that night, I was paraded into the Lieutenant's office, and each time he would offer me the piece of paper in his hand. "Sign, and go," he said the last time. This time he was not smiling. My skin was full of mosquito bites and I badly needed a shower. "NO!" I said with finality in my hoarse voice.

I was tired. The events of the day were taking its toll on me right now, and I realized that they were trying to play on my mind.

It was around five in the morning. Outside I heard the noise of traffic passing the little building I was in. A few dogs were barking in the distance and I could not help but to think about my sisters on the farm, as I was walked back to my cell a little while later.

My feet started to feel lazy and I was exhausted when I lay down on the cement bed on the one side of the cell. I turned my back to the wall and positioned the majority of the holes in the blanket over there, and drifted into a merciful sleep. I was not even aware of the fowl smell of the blanket anymore.

An hour later I was abruptly woken again, when someone dealt me a blow with his hand to the temple of my head.

A man whom I had not seen before was standing next to my bed. The blanket was pulled away from me and was lying on the floor. In the doorway were two women. For a few moments my head would not bring things into focus. It almost appeared as if my mind refused to wake up. Slowly, everything came together and I realized where I was and what was happening.

"Do you think you came here for a vacation?" the man asked me. The voices at first sounded like hollow echoes, but slowly, my mind started to put syllables together in sensible sentences.

"Get up you fool." The man barked out his commands and slowly I made my weary body get up from the hard, uncomfortable bed. I rose onto my weary feet, and the mosquito bites were itching all over. I scratched for a while and then realized that under these conditions infection would invariable set in. I forced my mind away from the desire to scratch and looked the man into the eyes.

"Follow me," and the man walked out of the cell into what seemed to be a kitchen area. The two women were standing there with a smile on their faces and at that moment my mind became alert.

I had heard how prisoners were raped in prison facilities such as these. With seventy percent of the adult population suffering from aids in this country, I told myself the previous night that should any of them attempt this vile act with me, I was going to fight to the death.

This life sentence was not going to be something I was ready to tolerate, and the old fighting spirit that used to be so much part of me in my earlier years now bounced back into my spirit. The adrenalin was pumping great amounts into my system and alertness caused my eyes to miss nothing.

My eyes took in my surrounding quick. There were two men and two women in this room. None of them were carrying any weapons. In the corner was a broom, which I could use effectively as a weapon. This was going to have to be a relentless attack. "I could not afford to show any mercy, and the man next to me was going to have to be the first to go."

My surprise knew no limits when the man next to me spoke with a little kindness in his voice, and told me to stand against the wall where a drain was visible on the floor.

"We heard what one of the men did to you last night, and we want to offer you a shower."

Remembering what had happened to me the night before, I did not know how to interpret the word "shower". The man lifted a short water hose from the sink and a sense of relief poured over me.

The cold, welcome shower brought freshness to my tired, yet alert senses. The two women stayed in the room, but I was beyond caring. I grabbed a cake of soap from the kitchen sink and when no one objected I washed and scrubbed. I enjoyed the moment and for a few moments I even felt like whistling my famous bathroom tune.

I still did not trust the situation, and while I was enjoying the ice cold shower, my eyes never missed a movement in the room.

At the end of the shower one of the women tossed my clothes to me and without asking for a towel I got into my shorts immediately in an attempt to finally cover my nakedness.

After getting the shirt over my wet body my surprise became even bigger when a warm cup of coffee was set in front of me.

The men and women were talking with each other and though I understood a large amount of what they were talking about I pretended not to understand at all. At one time one of the ladies asked me a question about my wife and family in her language but I pretended not to even notice she was talking to me and continued to sip my coffee.

After the coffee I was asked to turn right instead of left to my cell and once again was taken to another Lieutenant in the same office of the previous night.

The friendly man behind the desk invited me to sit down and for a while he talked to me about America and where I lived. He told me that he wanted to come there for a visit sometime, and all the while I knew that this was a different kind of setup. He was a very subtle man and it was not hard for me to notice this. I have been working and studying people all my life, and this man did not fool me.

On the untidy desk underneath a stack of loose paper I noticed a large nail clipper. "I need that thing," I said quietly to myself.

"Do you have a map for the United States?" I asked the man hoping that his attention would be drawn to somewhere else and I could get my hands on the clippers.

My plan worked like a charm and as he turned to get a map out of a filing cabinet behind him I reached the nail clippers without any problem. The clippers disappeared into my pocket, and for the next few minutes we talked about the USA. He asked me to show him where we lived and I cautiously indicated the wrong spot on the map. "You never know," I thought to myself.

Suddenly the man's demeanor changed as he came to the thing I have been waiting for. He pulled a drawer open on the side of his desk and came out with the same document the Lieutenant from the night before wanted me to sign.

"Mr. Venter," he said. "You and I have a good understanding. It seems as if we understand each other very well. This little form," and he lifted it up for me to look at, "is really a very innocent document. If you sign it we will have someone drop you off at the Sheraton Hotel in a few minutes."

The man was searching my face to see if he was getting through to me. I showed no expression of denial when I spoke calmly.

"Lieutenant, you are really a good man and I think the only sensible person I have met since my arrest." I paused and then continued as his face started to show some relief. "All of this will come to a neat end if you will allow me my rights as a United States Citizen and let me contact an attorney who can look that form through and should he agree with you that it was as innocent as you say, then I will sign it."

The real colors of the man jumped forward. He came out from behind his desk and cursed at me with spit flying in several directions. "You stubborn American capitalist. We will teach you lessons that you know nothing about. You don't even realize what we can do to you."

I realized that he was telling the truth. They are quite capable of the most violent actions, so I sat still and kept my eyes from making contact with him.

All I needed now was for them to take my clothes from me and the nail clippers would be discovered.

To my big relief I was commanded back to my cell without losing my clothes or this valuable piece of tool that was going to come in handy.

"No food for the prisoner," I heard the Lieutenant bark out the command. I did not care too much for the kind of food they would dish out to me anyhow, but I also knew that I would not be able to handle this kind of treatment indefinitely.

As soon as I came back to my cell, I went and sat around the corner against the wall where I took my little tool out of my pocket and investigated all its possibilities.

Carefully I dismantled the little tool and discovered that the various components could be turned into working tools for me should I want to escape.

The thought of escape was deliberately pushed out of my mind till now because of my two sisters on the farm.

Even if they did flee from Botswana, South Africa, under the new leadership of Mr. Mandela, would certainly extradite them and that would be fatal for the two frail ladies.

The thought of being sexually attacked was also not far from my mind and I decided that should things go in that direction I would have to be ready to escape.

Every hour the guards would come and bang against the door or do something to keep me awake. They were obviously not going to allow me any sleep. Several times during the day I was paraded back to the Lieutenants office, where we would go through the familiar routine of the night before. Each time I would shake my head and I would be paraded back to my cell. At times I would be kicked from behind or slapped on the back of the head.

"Keep your cool Yan," I would tell myself over and over. I knew I could handle this.

After each session I would go to work on the bars in front of the window sitting with my back to the door as if I was looking out. I had discovered a ledge on the outside where I would hide my tools between sessions.

At the end of the second day I had worked every screw loose where it was holding the bars. One hard push and the entire contraption would come loose. My plan was in place and I was ready to escape.

****

Four days dragged by but it felt as if it was four weeks that I was in that dreadful place.

My body was weak from not eating at all and the only time I had a drop of anything to drink, was the coffee from the first morning. My body was craving water but till now, I denied myself the water inside the cell. It was not clean in there and I was afraid of Cholera.

My skin was in poor condition from the repeated Mosquito attacks. I tried my best not to scratch, but when I was allowed to sleep, I would drift into short moments of bliss, and during these times I would discover afterwards that I had actually scratched my body. Invariably, infection started to set in and I was in bad need of basic treatment.

A few times I looked at the bars and considered my escape plans, but the thought of leaving my sisters in the lurch caused me to abandon the plan each time.

The weaker my body became, the more I became aware of the eminent danger. I realized that should an attack be made on me now, I would not have much strength left to fight them off, and if I waited too much longer, I would not have the strength to flee either.

"Tonight will be my last night here," I promised myself. "If something does not happen today, I am going to leave."

My knees had started to blister from the many occasions I had knelt on this rough floor to talk to the Lord.

Slowly I went down on my knees another time. Tears were flowing over my cheeks as I approached the Lord with the deepest sincerity.

"Lord, I know that Elizabeth and the rest of my family, have been trying to find me. It seems as if no one can find me and I am so weak."

Each time I pronounced a word, excruciating pain followed as my lips were so severely cracked. My shoulders started to shake and I was aware of someone watching me through the peephole in the door, but I continued my prayer.

"Lord, I know that I have failed you, but I repent before you today. I have asked you before to make me financially independent, and now I realize how wrong my prayers have been. Please Lord, make me dependant on you once again."

My prayer continued and suddenly the presence of the Lord filled the place. I was no longer alone in that filthy hole. God heard my prayer, and at that moment, I think I know what Samson felt like when God came and offered him a second chance.

"God, no one can find me here. These people have wicked intentions with me, but I turn myself back into your care.

With both my arms lifted up in total abandonment, I became aware of the Master's surrounding presence. Tears and laughter filled my spirit. I just knew that God was about to take this horrible wrench out of my hand.

I was ready. My miracle could not come one moment to soon because I was at the end of the line.

Suddenly, I heard the voice of a South African speak to my jailors in the front office, only a short distance from my cell. The thing that drew my attention was when this Samaritan from nowhere spoke and said, "I am an attorney, representing Mr. Yan Venter."

Cold chills ran over my body. "I was discovered!"

I jumped up from my knees and ran to the bars of my cell, grabbing them with both my hands until the white showed on my knuckles. My heart pounded in my chest and I tuned my ears to listen to every welcome sound of this friend from somewhere.

"We do not have any such person here," I heard my jailor lie to this attorney.

"That is a blatant lie sir. If you do not have Mr. Venter here, what is his briefcase doing there on your desk?"

My ostrich leather briefcase with my nametag inscribed on the front of it was lying on the man's desk and my bible with my name embossed on the front cover as an obvious indictment against this lying scoundrel.

The man looked down to the artifacts in front of him like a little child whose hand was caught in the cookie jar.

He stuttered as he attempted one more lie, by saying, "He was here, but they have moved him somewhere else."

Even though my body felt weak, and my blistered lips was hurting so badly, I started shouting at the top of my lungs like the blind Bartholomew of old. "I am here sir, he is lying to you!"

This tall, South African attorney responded immediately by saying, "Do you realize that you are illegally holding an American Citizen as prisoner without affording him his legal rights?"

Mr. Badenhorst a firm, but otherwise friendly attorney took his cell phone from his pocket and threatened to call the US Consulate.

My jailor immediately changed his manner of approach and lifted his hand up with an apologetic gesture and told Mr. Badenhorst that he first wanted to make a call to his superiors.

After just a few minutes, this small, arrogant jailor, who had caused me so much pain, hung the phone up and explained to the attorney with a fresh smirk on his face, "this is Botswana and you are not a registered attorney in this country."

My new attorney friend was not deterred at all and while my jailor was still speaking, he pressed a key on his cell phone and while the call was placed, he replied by saying "no problem my man, my colleague from Gaborone, Mr. Jeff Bookbinder will be here in only a few minutes."

In my small, stuffy jail cell, which felt more like a cage, I felt like jumping up an down with joy like a Chimpanzee.

Hansie Badenhorst planted himself outside the cheap Police Station with the promise to my jailor that he would not leave without his client.

Less than four hours later I sat in a restaurant with the two attorneys eating a hearty meal.

****

As I drove up to our farm, armed guards from the Government were at our gate. The farm had been temporarily seized and every move was carefully monitored.

Nothing could stop our workers from rejoicing as I drove into the yard. I noticed that the fires were ready to be lit. Sienie, Annie, Bertus and Barry were waiting for me. My friend Rock was standing under a tree allowing the family their right to greet me first. The buoyant atmosphere was undeniably present as I stepped out of the vehicle. It felt as if I was a general that had just returned from a hard fought battle.

Our black workers sang and danced in rhythmic unison as they declared their loyalty to Manie and me. I felt so proud and yet I missed home.

The government kept my passport and there was no way I could get out of the country.

"What are we going to do my boetie?" Sienie came and stood right beside me. Annie was on the other side. She hooked into my arm, with Sienie on the other side, and said: "We're going to fight them, Yan. We are not going to give in. They will pay dearly."

I looked over the kopje at the horizon, and there was not a cloud in the sky.

Not long and the flames of the African Campfire reached up high in the sky. The flames were almost typical of our spirits. Fired up and rearing to go.

EGGS WITH NO ASSIGNMENT

We could not trust any telephone lines at this time. The only phone we could possibly use was at the South African border control, and without a passport, I could not reach the outside world at all.

"Annie, will you go to the border control and get a hold of my friend Piet, the detective. Tell him I need him here by tomorrow."

An hour later, Annie arrived back on the farm. "He is already on his way Yan. As soon as he heard what had happened to you, he told me to let you know he will be here tonight."

It is truly amazing how your true friends appear around you at a time such as this. In the good times, you have so many that want to be around you, but now, only the ones who are true were showing their real colors.

Bernie and Adrie were already on the farm when I got there. My older sister Joey could not be kept away in spite of the fact that her kids advised her against such action because of lurking danger.

Bernie was like a pillar behind me and I decided that if there will ever be a time I can pay these people back in kindness, I will not leave a stone unturned.

When the army of raiders came to the farm, they made sure all our records were taken, but they did not keep track with the effectiveness of Annie and Sienie, who made regular backups of all records, which was kept separate.

Proudly, Annie and Sienie escorted me into our raided office. No paper work of any kind was left behind. The place was in shambles but in a secret place in the addict, my two sisters now proudly produced these records to me. "It is all there Yan," Annie said to me with pride in her eyes. "They thought they removed all evidence of what we had, but they failed. We have it all here," she said while she held the floppy diskettes and paper work to her bosom and tapped them lightly with her fingertips.

Both my sisters smiled at me while their eyes revealed the fighting spirit, which is so common in both of them.

Sienie waited her turn and then jumped in as soon as Annie paused to take a breath. "We have a lawsuit here my boetie. Annie and I started with a journal right away from the first moment these men walked into our lives, and I promise you that I will faithfully keep these journals till it is all done.

Early the following morning, Piet, the detective arrived on the farm just as he promised.

"Did I warn you about these men, or what?" This tall man with the strong Eastern Cape accent, stood in front of me and his very presence brought a strange calmness to my spirit. Piet was a walking dictionary. He knew all the right people.

For the next hour I sat down and filled him and all the people on the farm in on the events of the past few days. The anger and amazement were seen on everyone's face as I told them about our shipment of eggs that were being kept in Gaborone.

The shipment was worth a fortune and was kept in storage under false indictments.

"It was a matter that would have to be dealt with in court, Mr. Venter," my attorney told me in Gaborone before I returned to the farm. He explained that we would have to appeal to the Supreme Court of Botswana and though it would cost a small fortune in itself, this would be the only way to go.

We were also advised to get a hold of the "real" shipment of eggs in Ellisras and preserve it in its original state, for that moment when we would present that evidence in court.

Because none of those eggs were going to be exported, they were never washed and therefore we knew that any of those markings, which these hoodlums placed on the eggs after we purchased them in the Cape, would still be visible.

Piet interrupted me as I told everyone about the false indictments and he said: "Well, those eggs must not hatch then. I suggest I collect them for keeping in a safe place."

My focus in life returned around the campfire that night. Soberness of mind came back with the help of these friends. I was once again able to pull myself together. Everyone shared his or her opinion, and by the time the evening was over, we already had the President and his hoodlums in jail, as far as our little group was concerned.

The guards of the President that were placed in and around the farm to harass us did not intimidate anyone. Our workers openly ignored them and deliberately did not supply them with any food or water.

Sienie started her journal and every detail was carefully noted. Annie and Rock fine combed all our records, and on a regular basis backups were made. No chances were taken at any time and while they worked on the records, someone was placed on guard duty. It was their responsibility to notify us of any approaching enemy. The records would then be hidden in a safe place. We realized that should these thugs find them, we would loose them also.

The long task of giving trace to each egg had begun, and now more than ever before, I appreciated Annie's diligence to have her records so much in order.

Rock was deathly afraid of his own safety. He would stand behind me no matter what, but after hearing about the ordeal I went through in jail, he made us promise that as soon as the enemy arrived, we would give him enough time to hide somewhere in the house.

"They're at the gate Rock," Annie teased our goodly accountant and immediately he jumped through the side window of the office, leaving everything behind. Before anyone could stop this fearful friend, he disappeared into the main house, hiding himself behind Sienie's dresser.

The office staff, roared with laughter, knowing that Annie was playing a joke on him. After only a few minutes, Annie followed him into the room with persistence. There was no trace of a smile on her face when she whispered in an urgent tone to the thin, scared man behind the dresser to come out as the Department of Wildlife saw him with their binoculars and now wanted to question him.

Rock started shaking all over and as he rose up from his hiding place, his eyes were white in their sockets and his hair was badly out of place. He looked a real mess and had the appearance of someone who saw a ghost.

Although he was quaking like a dead man with even his dentures knocking up and down inside his mouth, the mischievous Annie carried her foul play a little further by saying to our shaking friend, "Don't worry Rock, we will all stand with you."

Only when she decided he suffered enough, she came out with the truth. Rock broke out in tears and for the next few days he wouldn't talk to Annie.

A few nights later, Rock and me decided it was payback time. The two ladies were calmly sitting in the sitting room doing needlework, while Bertus was trimming his beard and Barry was lying on the bed watching TV. The atmosphere was tranquil when all of a sudden pandemonium broke loose.

My voice came through on the two-way radio with clarity. Everyone felt the urgency of the moment when I announced that I was at the neighbor's house and in serious need of urgent assistance. Suddenly, everyone went into spontaneous action. Even though Bertus suggested that he go there alone, my two sisters would know nothing of it. "All for one and one for all," Annie barked out her orders like a Sergeant Major while Sienie moved in behind her like a shadow, ready to follow.

Just as they were ready to leave, Sienie remembered that Barry was still on the bed. In a frantic manner she turned and reached his room in a few long strides. While she instructed her husband to move quick, she also reached for two valiums and instructed him to swallow it without water. The poor husband had no idea what was happening but he also realized that drastic measures were now being followed. He ran out behind Sienie without shoes and jumped on the back of the pick-up and this small army made their rush for the gate, only to find Rock and me there, doubling up with laughter.

Ten minutes later when everything had returned to normal, poor ol' Barry was fast asleep as a result of the two valiums.

Marina, the neighbor's daughter in law was vehemently opposed to the dirty tricks the government was playing on us. She and her husband have proven themselves as great friends and during this time no stone was left unturned in order to assist us in every possible way.

Her car came through the gate and the way she stopped, told us that she had something to tell us. The dust filled the entire backyard. She didn't waste anytime and hurried into our little office. The door was carefully closed behind her, and then she asked: "Is it safe for me to talk in this room?" We all smiled and I realized what great stress this drama has brought even upon our friendly neighbors.

With a dry smile, she said: "Well, you never know if this room is bugged. These thugs will stop at nothing.

"Relax," Annie told her. "Piet, our detective friend, fine combed the entire house. We are clean. What do you have on your heart?"

Regardless of our assurance, she continued in a secretive whisper. "Piet called, and said for me to tell you that he picked up all the groceries you asked for. He said that he has it out of the freezer, and in a safe place. The entire list of groceries is coded as you suspected," she said.

Marina paused for a moment with a frown on her forehead. "Does that make any sense to you?"

We smiled and nodded our heads. No further information was volunteered and she accepted it as such.

Piet's message made perfect sense. The eggs from Ellisras have been picked up and the markings on them were confirmed as we suspected.

The war was on. The sparks were going to fly and someone was going to be held responsible. "El Presidente, you and your mob have gotten yourselves into a mess you may regret," I said silently to myself.

SUPREME COURT

Nothing in this country is for sure. We already found that out and even in the courts where I appeared briefly to have my bond set, Mr. Bookman alerted me to this fact.

"How certain are you that we will get a fair ruling from the Supreme Court, Mr. Bookman?" Annie asked the short Canadian Attorney, who was brave enough to take this case on when it seemed as if no other wanted it.

We were assured that these men on the bench of the Supreme Court were men of the law with great integrity.

The atmosphere inside the courtroom was tense. The most up and coming Prosecuting Attorney was appointed against us and it was immediately obvious that he had his gun in for us.

It was going to be of utmost importance for him to see us at the shortest end. His own future was very much at stake.

Mr. Bookman retained the services of a brilliant Advocate from Johannesburg, in the Republic of South Africa.

The man was a brain in two shoes. He knew the law on the tips of his fingers and the previous day, as we met with him and our Attorney in his office, it was obvious that the man knew what he was talking about.

Not much was said by any of us the day before, and this morning as we sit in this Courtroom, no one was talking at all. We were all making observations of our surroundings.

The Court was situated far outside the skirts of the city. The building on the outside was not like your typical Supreme Court setting. We were told that the Supreme Court was under construction, and therefore they moved into prefabricated buildings where the court proceedings would be held.

Inside the Courtroom, the normal setting was in place. The bench of "your honor" was large. Almost too large for the small room we were in.

The few seats at the back of the room were hardly enough for Sienie, Annie and me to sit in. Several flies zoomed around in this musky room.

Our Advocate walked into the room and sat down, deliberately ignoring the Prosecutor. They exchanged glances followed by professional smiles, and after a little while, the Prosecutor walked over to our man.

Our Attorney was not in a jovial mood. It was not long before it seemed to us as if the court case began even before the judge came out of his quarters. These two legal giants engaged in a legal argument.

The three of us were sitting there pretty nervous as these two advocates sparred with each other. No friendly words were forthcoming and our representative did not back down an inch. I did not know if I should admire him or be concerned, because the Prosecutor was fighting mad.

The small door behind the desk opened and the Sergeant At Arms announced that "his honor" was about to make his entrance.

The eyes of everyone turned towards the door and order was restored in the court. The two Advocates gathered their papers and notes together and I could not help but to notice that they were both nervous. The air was tense and so were we.

There was so much at stake. Since my arrest, the department of Wildlife informed us that all export permits had been revoked, and the guards at the gate to our farm were engaging in horrible acts of intimidation.

We could not afford to maintain our farm for too long without overseas exports. The ostriches were eating twenty tons of feed each two weeks. The salaries of the large staff were enormous and the demands from our investors were putting so much stress on all of us.

This was going to be a test on the integrity of the court. "Could it be possible that this old man seated behind the bench could have enough authority to overrule this series of events against us?" I thought to myself.

The Judge was a white man and quite old. I estimated his age to be very deep into his seventies. There was no sign of any mental weakness in him, as he engaged in legal debate with our Advocate. Then he also listened attentively to the arguments of the Prosecutor.

It soon became evident to us that the old man was going to make his decision based on the law.

Nothing was out of place and no one spoke out of turn. The events in the courtroom were a perfect example of authority and though I was still nervous, a calm assurance had come over my spirit. Sienie and I looked at each other and smiled. I knew that she felt the same.

One more time the Prosecutor stood up to present his case but then the aged judge silenced him outright and said: "Sit down. I have heard enough. I don't need any more time to make up my mind."

The stern old man looked at us over the small reading glasses on his long European nose. He spoke to me, and said: "You have not been treated well and I hereby issue an order for those guards to get off your property immediately. When you get to your farm, you tell them that I said this. It is going to take a while for this court order to be typed out, but if they have any problem with this verbal order, let them call my office."

The Prosecutor stood up to address the old Judge, but the wise old man, waved him down with his hand, and when the man still did not seem to get the message, the Judge brought his anvil down hard on the bench and said: "Not a further word will be said on this matter. This matter is now closed, and you will see to it that all guards be removed from their farm and that all export permits be restored."

With that final word the judge got up and walked out of the courtroom before any person could get to their feet in time.

Relief spilled over me. I laughed out loud and Sienie and Annie jumped up and down with glee.

198

The prosecutor stood with his head hanging and our Advocate turned his back abruptly on the man and walked over to us.

"You go and tell those hoodlums to get off your farm right now," he said.

"Nothing will give us more pleasure sir," Sienie talked over my shoulder before I could say anything.

"What about my passport and the indictments against me?" I asked the smiling Advocate.

"No, that matter will have to be resolved in the lower court where it started but believe me they do not have a case now that the Supreme Court have ruled in your favor."

He continued to explain how pleasantly surprised he was about the ruling, since such "high powers" were acting against us.

We drove the horrible four-hour journey back to our farm with excitement in our hearts. The roads were the worst I have seen since the rains fell. All the way there, we spoke and reminisced about the events of that morning.

Before we left for the farm, I headed to the office of the man who headed the raid on our farm and whose men were now still on our property. Our attorney informed me to do this and suggested if Wildlife had any questions, they should contact the office of the prosecutor.

I ran up the stairs to the 3rd floor of this dirty building. There was a new spring in my step and I felt better than in a long time.

The door of the man's office was open and I walked in boldly. When I addressed the man in charge, I was sarcastically friendly. "Sir, I just come from the Supreme Court, where the Judge issued an order for you to get your men off our property."

The eyes of this unfriendly man who reminded me of Idi Amin from Uganda, opened up real big, and he sneered some disrespectable remark back at me.

"No, I am only the messenger of the court sir," and I continued to tell him that he was suppose to contact the prosecutor if he did not believe my report.

When I walked out of the office, I felt good. I enjoyed the surprise in the man's eyes.

The hard four-hour ride passed by before we noticed it, and we finally drove up the one and a half mile driveway to our gate.

Our surprise was great when we noticed the same activity at our gate. The guard walked around to my side of the vehicle, but I refused to answer any of his intimidating questions.

"You are now illegal on my property," I told the man, and demanded that he contact his superior in Gaborone.

I drove away from the angry soldier and left him standing at the open gate. Bertus, Barry and Rock, were standing in the yard of the farm waiting for news. We were unable to hide our excitement as we stopped and immediately their faces showed relief.

A couple of minutes later, the noise of several army vehicles were heard starting up and they drove off our land. We rejoiced, and some of our workers lifted their fists up in the air after them.

CHAPTER 5

THE WRENCH HANDED BACK

CROCODILE WATERS

The farm was buzzing with activity. Things had almost returned to normal except for the fact that we still had a war on our hands.

My wife had come for a short visit to Botswana and the moment she stepped out of the car, we were in each other's arms without shame or consideration of others.

She kissed me on the cheeks, on my arms and everywhere she could possibly get a place to fit a kiss. She was crying through a smile and her tears illuminated the sparkle that for years had kept butterflies going in my stomach.

The moment was sweet, and for a while I had to fight tears away myself.

All those around us respected the moment and patiently waited for their turn to greet her also.

Bontshe in the Tuli Block, had suddenly become attractive to me, and as I stepped back to let the others greet Elizabeth, I caught the eye of my friend, Rock, who winked at me with approval as if to say: "Now you are complete again."

At that moment I felt as if I could jump over a wall and storm a troop, like King David once said.

I suddenly felt young again, and I was amazed at the rush of adrenaline that this little lady's presence had brought into my spirit. "What a friend she had proven herself to be through the years," I thought to myself as I watched her laugh out loud among all the family.

The events of the past weeks had left deep marks of stress on the face of this little lady of mine. Through the years she had proven herself as strong as a tree with deep roots. This time was no exception and no distance could keep her from coming to stand at my side.

An hour later, the guard at the heavy gate, lending entrance into our yard, pushed it open and smiled a friendly greeting with his hat in his hands.

As we walked past him, he spoke to me in his language, and said: "Bwana, now you are a lion again. Your blood will be strong and your mind will be open." I laughed as I agreed with him, and although Elizabeth did not understand the language, she did not question me. Instead, she looked up and said: "They love you, Yan."

We walked slow, hand in hand and we talked and visited. Too much time had gone by and when we got to the end of the road, we sat down under a strong and proud Jakkalsbessie tree. (A jackal Berry tree) She laid her back against mine, and while we supported our backs against each other, we emptied our hearts. I let her do it first. I realized that she had much to say, and for the next hour she spoke with strength in her voice. There were no accusations, there were no anger, but while she spoke, the strength of her spirit lifted me.

Though I could not see her face, I knew that she was not blinking. She was not voicing an opinion. No. She was talking to me in a way that only she could.

I told her how God found me on my knees in the Botswana jail, and shamelessly, I cried softly. She never interrupted me for a moment. "I am done here baby. As soon as this court case is over I am handing everything over to Manie and the others."

Elizabeth reached around her back and gave my arm a reassuring squeeze.

I explained to her that the only thing that stood in my way to walk away at that moment was the fact that the lower court had not concluded their case against me yet.

My emotions were trying to run away from me and Elizabeth realized that the moment embarrassed me. Suddenly, she got up from behind and playfully allowed me to fall over backwards. Like two little children we played for a while and I chased her around the tree a few times until I caught her around the waist and in abandonment she threw herself against me. Slowly she turned and faced me. Her arms came around my neck in a loving embrace and I pulled her tight against me.

The old feeling of butterflies in the stomach came back and I held her in my embrace while turtledoves sung for us in the surrounding trees.

****

The department of wildlife showed open aggression toward us when I walked into their office to ask for our export permit for the next batch of eggs.

Defiantly, the lady behind the desk told me that there was a "higher power" against us and that they were told not to give me the permit, which was ordered by the Supreme Court.

A few weeks earlier we were told that the old Judge had reported sick and no one knew when he would be back on duty.

Mr. Bookman looked me in the eyes and said: "Yan, we are dealing with dangerous forces here, and we have to move slow." The courts were still holding my passport and the Advocate in Johannesburg needed to see me, I was told.

"Somehow, you need to get to Johannesburg," he told me. "So much had to be prepared for our case and the matter of your eggs in South Africa need to be discussed in detail."

"We will need to apply for your passport to be handed back to you the next time we are in court, but for now, we have to just wait our turn." The Attorney told me as a matter of fact.

Mr. Bookman did not want to know how I was going to get into South Africa, and I was not going to volunteer the information either. I first had to take this matter under serious consideration because I did not want to do anything at this stage of my life, unless God was giving me peace in my spirit.

When I arrived back at the farm, Rock and I discussed the matter carefully. There was only one place I could cross, and it was not safe.

I had to cross over the crocodile infested river, and the only place that was safe enough as far as the enemy was concerned, was at a place where the water was calm.

The only problem was that crocodiles don't like fast waters. The calm waters at the potential crossing point were bound to have several of these reptiles and the crossing had to take place at night. No flashlights could be used for fear of being seen.

Rock was not keen on my idea at all.

"Is there no boat that we could use?" he asked the question that was first in his mind.

I told him there was a man in that area who owned a small boat, but could not be trusted.

"What I am going to do tonight Rock, is to go and check the place out. If my heart feels good about the crossing, then I am going to do it right away. You can follow if you want to, but I will not hold it against you should you decide not to go. It is going to be very dangerous and possibly the wildest thing you have ever done in your life." I smiled at him when I said this.

"You don't have to tell me that my friend. Look, if there is anything I am very afraid of, it is Crocodiles. Those things are afraid of nothing, and the moment you get into that water brother, they will eat you!"

Rock was talking loud. He was as serious as I had ever seen him. His hands moved wildly in front of him as he spoke and his glasses had to be set a few times while he was talking.

Unlike Alligators, Crocodiles look at humans as part of their food chain. They display no fear at all.

"You are not normal Yan, you know that." I could not help but to laugh at the seriousness with which Rock was talking to me. "I know that you are a man of faith, but this one beats anything I have ever heard you do.

In the history of stupid acts, this one is a humdinger.

Rock had to be in the meeting with the Attorneys also. He fully recognized that I had to cross the border and there was not really any other alternative. However, this good friend of mine was not happy at all.

Next to my own family, Rock, possibly knew me better than anyone else I know. He was now frantically trying to convince me about how ludicrous my plan was.

He is one of the best friends I have ever had and will walk through fire with me, but this one, was asking a little too much from him.

For the next hour, Rock, came up with one idea after another but all of them just did not make sense and finally he agreed to go with me that night "to check things out."

He made sure I understood, that we were only going to the water "to check things out."

We drove our car as close to the water as possible without using lights. It was a cloudy night and no stars were visible at all.

A strange silence was hanging in the air between the two of us and even though no one could hear our conversation in the car, whenever one of us would say anything, it would be in a whisper.

As we quietly stepped out of the car, I thought to myself that this was one of the darkest nights I had ever seen. This was one night I was in need of the moon, but it was not available.

The place was spooky and some heavy weight frogs were sounding out their ugly gurgling sounds.

This moment was not for the weak and knowing what I was about to do, caused me to hesitate for just a moment. As I stopped to think about my actions, Rock bumped into my back.

My friend was breathing loud behind me. We had both been very active in the Rhodesian war and we had been involved in some tight situations, but nothing could match the tension we both felt at that moment.

This was danger in a raw sense of the word. I abandoned the thought of fear from my mind and moved closer to the water.

Rock pulled at my shirt from behind. "Wait... where are you going?" He asked in a loud whisper.

"I am going to the water," I said, and tried to walk a little further, but Rock had me in a firm grip on my arm.

"You haven't prayed yet," he said with alarm. I thought I heard a quiver in his voice and realized that the tension was also running high in him.

I felt the tension myself, but I had already prayed about the matter and decided to make the crossing. I only did not say anything to my friend, Rock.

I turned to him and without asking him to close his eyes I started praying in a loud whisper.

"Father," I said: "Thank you that you are alive in my spirit and that I can believe you for a moment like this. You know that I have to get to the other side tonight, and Lord, there is no other way for me to do it than this."

Rock was quiet next to me till then. He was holding my hand in a strong grip. All of a sudden he joined my prayer and prayed the things that he thought I was not confessing to: "Father, please also tell this good friend of mine that we are not suppose to tempt the Lord our God."

I could not help but to smile, and for a moment I almost giggled. I suppressed the desire to smile and then continued my prayer as if I was in a debate with Rock before the Lord.

"Father, there was a time when Shadrack, Meshack and Abednego needed your help, and then there was Daniel in the lion's den," and I continued to remind Rock in my prayer that the same God who performed those great miracles for men of faith in the past, was also now standing with us on the banks of this dark, dangerous river.

As if Rock realized that he was not going to win, he remained silent until I said: "Amen," to my prayer. Only then did he slowly release my arm, and said in a normal tone.

"You have decided to cross haven't you Yan?" I nodded my head, but then realized he could not see that motion, and I answered with a convincing: "Uhu."

"Well, I haven't heard God speak to me, so, I don't think I will go with you,"

The moment of truth arrived for me. If I did not have Rock with me to remind me so eloquently of the stupidity of my act, it would have been easier. Now, my mind was filled with fear and suspicion of the unknown.

Crocodiles were definitely in the water but I could not see them and this made the moment even tenser.

I moved up to the water, stood still for just a little while, and then put fear to the side. I stepped into the cool, dark waters.

The water was cold and a shock to my already tense system. At first it was only ankle deep, then a little deeper and further, and suddenly I stepped into a deep place and had to swim. I tried not to make any noise at all but suddenly I heard something behind me.

It was the stirring noise of water, and at that moment my heart missed a few beats and almost stopped.

I turned to face whatever was coming up behind me. At first I could not make out what it was, but to my great surprise it was Rock. He wasn't saying anything but I was almost in a state of shock. My mouth tasted like salt and the adrenaline rush in my body was almost more than I could bear.

I waited until he was close to me and then continued.

No words can explain the pride I felt at that moment, when this good friend of mine, appeared behind me like that.

He also conquered his fear, and later told me: "I was not going to allow you to outdo me with your faith. I said to myself, 'if he can do it, so can I.'"

As we stepped out of the water on the other side we fell down on our knees and thanked God for this miracle, and then we laughed lightheartedly.

We laughed out loud and giggled like two young teenagers. The relief we felt was incredible and it bubbled out of our mouths.

"I wish I could have seen the expression in your eyes the moment you turned around to see what was coming behind you," Rock said through an almost hysterical laughter.

We realized that this was no small accomplishment, and not just any ordinary person would have carried out this crazy task.

Several days later when we returned, we found someone on the other side to help us out with a boat and we crossed the river during daytime.

As we steered the boat to the other side, our eyes were piercing the waters and it was not long before we noticed several large crocodiles on the opposite side, slip silently into the water and disappeared from sight.

Rock and I exchanged glances of relief with one another, but said nothing until we finally sat in our car on the opposite side.

"Wow," Rock said as he wiped a cold sweat from his brow. "That is the wildest thing I had ever done in my entire life."

We laughed again, but before we drove off back to the farm, we prayed again and thanked God for His Hand of protection upon our lives.

POISON IN THE FOOD

"Bwana, Bwana," Johannes cried out while he was banging on the back door of the house.

Bertus jumped up behind the kitchen table where we were enjoying our morning coffee.

We had just finished our quiet time and were singing the final line of our chorus. Rock was playing his guitar and I was leading the little group in worship.

Johannes was frantically calling out for us and as we stepped out behind Bertus, his arms was swinging wide, his eyes were white and he was talking a mixture of his language and English together. Nothing he said was making sense, and Bertus had to silence him first.

"Something serious must be going on," I said to myself and many thoughts were racing through my mind. I had no idea what to expect. At this point in my life I was expecting anything. Nothing could surprise me anymore.

Johannes took a deep breath, Bertus, stood calmly in front of him with his pipe in his mouth and then this good worker of ours started talking again.

"Bwana, the Ostrich. They are dead. Many of them are dead. Others are dying and something terrible had happened."

Cold fingers gripped my heart. We all followed Bertus, as he started to run after Johannes, to the

Pickup that was parked beneath the big tree in the backyard.

Everyone jumped on the back and as we drove in among the camp, birds were lying all around. Some were turning around in circles, while others were kicking on the ground and others were already dead.

"When did this start Johannes?" Bertus was frantic like all of us. "This morning Bwana. This morning, just as we started to feed the birds."

The new feed was delivered only a few days earlier, and Bertus knew they started on the new batch of feed that morning.

"Get the feed away from the birds." Bertus cried out.

All of us went into action. The remains of the feed in the barrels on the ground were pulled outside the camps.

There was nothing we could do for the poor birds. The ones that have eaten of the feed were dying.

Only the top camps had received feed, when Johannes noticed that something eerie was happening.

By the end of the day pandemonium had broken loose. Several hundred birds were dead.

We called for a research company from South Africa to come to our aid. The next morning, as soon as the border gates opened, they came through to our farm.

The atmosphere was gloomy once again. No one was smiling and very little was said. All night long, the previous evening, we speculated about the causes, but now we resigned ourselves to this fateful event. The research team was at work. A mile outside the camp we had made a huge fire, and some of our top birds were now being burned.

Sienie and Annie cried as if someone in the family had passed away, and the workers were standing around in total shock as we poured more oil on the dead carcasses for the fire to consume them entirely.

The rest of the birds in the camps were restless. They were hungry, but we had decided not to carry on with this batch of feed till we were sure what was going on.

Bertus had already contacted a neighboring Ostrich farmer who expressed willingness to help with feed for the birds, once we found out what was going on.

Two hours after this team arrived on the farm, the leader of this highly professional team, called Bertus and I to their little laboratory they had set up in the yard.

"Mr. Stieler," he said to Bertus with a worried look in his eyes. We took several tests from one of the dead birds. The results were truly amazing, sir." He paused for a moment to let his statement sink in deep within our minds. "Your birds have been deliberately poisoned."

"Poisoned?" Bertus pulled his pipe from his mouth and we both shouted the question out together. "How in the world could they have been poisoned? What kind of poison? How did it get there?" Bertus rattled the questions out one after another without waiting for an answer.

The manager of this scientific team lifted his hand for us to be quiet so that he could offer the answers to our many questions.

"After discovering the presence of Arsenic in these birds, we tested your water as well as the feed." He walked over to his field laboratory and we followed him automatically without saying a word.

He took some feed in his hand from the table and said: "Here is your problem. Your feed has been poisoned and by the looks of it we would say that it is deliberate."

Bertus and I stood stunned in silence. "Who would do something so cruel?" Bertus asked, and while he didn't expect an answer we knew that Piet's warning was ringing out to us.

"You have dangerous people as your enemies."

The feed company was from South Africa. The owners of that company were also the corporate owners of some of the largest Ostrich farms in the world.

Hansie Badenhorst, together with our advocate, immediately filed a law suite against this wicket group of people. We were assured that this was going to be an easy win. I realized at that time, I was not going to carry on with this wrench in my hand and the matter would be handed over to Manie and the attorneys.

We burned our birds, changed our feed company and lifted our heads once again to face another tomorrow.

One thing was for sure; I was no longer interested in this business. My mind was made up. "I am going home, and Manie can have this all for himself.

GUILTY BUT NOT GUILTY

The Courtroom was packed with curious individuals and reporters. This was the day we were all looking forward to.

We had all done our homework well. For several weeks we worked hard on our records and tried to cover every detail that could possibly be asked in court.

Two weeks after the prosecutor from this lower court learned that the government had lost their case in the Supreme Court, they showed up on the farm and laid charges on my two sisters and their husbands.

They knew that they would not be able to deny me the right of my passport and by doing this they would have some sort of control over me.

Sitting in the courtroom now was a representative of the American Consulate, the two policemen from South Africa who was involved in this scam, and a few other people we did not know, were there.

All five of us were directed to a long bench that had been specially placed there to accommodate all of us.

We sat down and looked over to our legal team who had taken their place in court.

The prosecutor was an arrogant little man who reminded me of a fox terrier dog trying to take on a bulldog in a fight.

The little that I spoke to the man I could tell that he would be no match for these giants in the law, which we hired.

Now, as everyone took their positions it became increasingly noticeable of the contrast between these teams. Our legal team had their table stacked with materials and files of all sorts, while the prosecutor only had a thin manila folder lying in front of him on the table.

As I sat there waiting for the Judge to show up, I allowed my mind to go over the events of the past few weeks.

The Advocate interviewed Piet extensively about the eggs that were now in his possession. In the presence of another South African officer they inspected the eggs with a video camera present and rolling at all times. He testified under oath that they discovered all the eggs were marked with infrared markings and that the same boxes, which were used to pack the eggs in from Ellisras, were in his possession.

"Did you tell anyone about this?" The Advocate asked Piet and looked over to me for the same answer. "No sir," Piet answered and I also shook my head in agreement.

The Advocate said: "I want to hit them hard with this evidence at the right time."

Piet assured him that he would be in the courtroom for the case and as we were sitting in court, it was so good to see this tall man there. He kept his promise and as I sat looking in his direction, he winked at me in a reassuring way.

All of us were well prepared. For several weeks now we took turns to play the role of a mean prosecutor and had our own court sessions on the farm. Bertus and Barry were drawn in at the end of every day's work, and we relentlessly worked on both of them, until they became irritated with us.

Sienie was concerned with Barry folding under the pressure in court, and so we worked extra hard on him, until we thought he was as smooth as a baby's bottom.

Every bit of detail was worked on and now as we sat in court we had stacks of records in front of us also, that we could make reference to during the proceedings.

If they wanted a war we were ready and looking forward to the opening bell of this sparring match.

We started the morning by having breakfast with our legal team. I made sure that the spirits of everyone remained high. We were a team and I was going to make sure that it stayed that way till the end.

I had already booked my ticket back to the United States, and told myself that I would walk away from all of this following the proceedings. "As soon as this court case was over, I was going to get back to normal, " I said to myself.

I wanted to get back into the ministry which I hadn't had time for, now for almost two years.

A small, old man, opened the door behind the Judge's desk and announced loud that the District Judge was about to enter.

The prosecutor looked over to me and he had a mean expression in his eyes. I did not back down an inch and stared straight back at this thin, sickly looking individual.

The fight had begun and we were ready for the punches to roll. The Judge leaned forward and looked at the prosecutor. "Are you ready to proceed?"

With a sneer on his face the prosecutor got up and said, "Your honor, the state is not ready to proceed. Due to the international nature of this case, we are still busy with our investigation and therefore request a continuance."

We sat there stunned. No one could believe his or her ears. Every thing came to an abrupt halt and there was nothing that anyone could do. The Advocate continued to appeal to the Court for the return of my passport and told the Judge that because of our investment here, and also my family members working for me, I would certainly not miss any future court appearance. The case was postponed for thirty days and we walked out with our heads hanging.

With my passport finally in my hands after the morning court-session, I made my way to the airport.

Sienie, Annie, Bertus and Barry, became known as my A-team, and as I boarded the airplane, the sad little group waved me off on my way home.

I was glad to go but at the same time, sad to leave them behind. I knew how hard it was going to be for them over the next few weeks.

The four weeks at home was like heaven for me. I busied myself by making contact once again with my friends in the church. It was not easy to just walk away like I wanted to, but I was trying hard to keep my promise to God which I had made on my knees in jail.

With the way things were developing, I remained in the business until the next court date. I was adamant to walk away as soon as the proceedings would come to an end.

Manie was content with my decision and all I had to do was to go back to Botswana one more time to get this matter resolved.

The month at home was spent getting my life back in order. Pastors were glad to hear from me again, and I started scheduling future meetings.

There was a sense of finality in my heart as I traveled back to Botswana.

As the big Boeing 747 landed at Jan Smuts, I sighed a sigh of relief. I have never been one for flying these long flights. Even though it was a direct flight from Miami, it still took seventeen hours for us to reach Johannesburg where I had to make another connecting flight to Botswana.

Irritated at the system for bringing me back so soon against my wishes, I boarded the old Botswana-Air Aircraft. It was an old propelled airplane and very noisy.

The air was thick with moisture and the airplane shook and creaked through all the air pockets and by the time we reached Gaborone, I was not feeling good at all.

The A-team waited for me at the airport and with real excitement welcomed me back in their midst.

Cheers went up as I stepped through the door and everyone grabbed my luggage and headed straight for the door.

"We've booked into the same Sheraton Hotel again Yan," Annie said. On the way to the hotel they took turns to fill me in on what is taking place on the farm.

As we walked into the hotel lobby, the two hoodlums from before were sitting there watching us as we entered. Sienie was the first to notice them, and shamelessly started mocking them until they got up and left the lobby, irritated by her open disdain.

"Well, what do you think will happen this time?" I asked Mr. Bookman when I called him from the hotel room.

He did not sound too convinced that things will be finalized and told me not to be too disappointed when it does not happen.

The following morning the Judge once again asked the Prosecutor, "Well, is the State ready to proceed?" The little sickly looking Prosecutor got up from his chair lazily, and said, "Your honor, this case is going to take a while because we have to investigate in so many parts of the world, and we ask for another continuance."

Our Attorneys attempted a weak protest but to no avail. The case was postponed for another thirty days!

This happened for seventeen more months! Seventeen months while nothing was allowed out of the farm as far as exports were concerned.

Seventeen months of the worst financial suffering imaginable. Each time, the Attorney's had to be paid, air tickets, hotels, salaries on the farm, feed for the animals and frustration at home.

Seventeen months later, I took the frustrated Mr. Bookman by the hand and said: "I don't care what you do, but you let that Judge know this matter ends today! I am not coming back here one more time. Not one more time!" I almost yelled the final sentence out into his face. I was frustrated and mad.

"I serve notice on you today, and on the court, that I am not coming back here again. You finalize this matter today or else you will not see me here one more time. I am through with Botswana. I am through with this Kangaroo Court and I am through with having to pay Attorney fees, and nothing is happening." The finality in my voice brought Mr. Bookman to where he stared at me and said: "I don't blame you Mr. Venter. I would do the same as you."

The telephone rang in my room at the Sheraton Hotel. The entire staff knew us by our first names by now. We had a regular suite on the third floor. We did not even book a room anymore. They knew we would be back.

I answered the phone and it was Mr. Bookman. He did not sound too excited.

"Yan, I spoke to the Prosecuting Attorney. They are willing to drop all charges against all of you. Your sisters and their husbands can walk away free. You will have to plead guilty to a minor offense of failing to complete the correct forms for exports.[12] That way you don't have to come back again."

I smiled by myself. "So, they do win after all," I spoke out aloud. "Well, if we don't do this there is no telling how long they can still drag this matter out.

"Go ahead Mr. Bookman. Close this matter. I want to go home." I told him in an abrupt manner and hung the phone up.

In the bathroom, I knelt down on my knees where there was privacy, and prayed: "Father, I hand this wrench back to you. I confess that I failed to get this nut loose. I humbly ask you to receive this tool back from me and allow me to now walk away from all of this. I want to be dependant on you again."

Suddenly, a peace came over my spirit. It felt as if a burden lifted from my shoulders and as I walked back into the room where everyone was waiting for me to tell them what was going to happen the next day, I felt good.

I was totally content the next day to close this matter once and for all. Everything came to a

---

[12] This referred to our first batch, which was exported, and the delay that was caused by the Custom Officials that day.

sudden halt. The nightmare was over and I threw this load off my shoulder.

Sitting on the Boeing 747 and listening to the engines starting up, I readied myself for the final flight home.

The case was shut down that morning and we ended a chapter in my life that never should have been written in the first place.

Africa had lost its attraction for me. I did not even pay a last visit to the farm. I was through. Manie and Bertus could carry the farm where they wanted.

****

Five years have passed. Like a young child I had to learn all over how to walk again. For a little while the Holy Spirit allowed me to start right at the bottom of the ladder, but now I have climbed the ladder of God's will higher than ever before.

My family and I walked away from all that used to be attractive to us. Not one dime was brought into our restored lives from the business. I handed the wrench back to my Father, and I was through with all of the past.

As I write this book my life is not only restored as an anointed man of God, but also restored in every financial way possible.

This book is meant to glorify the God of my salvation, and to bring warning to anyone who wishes to pursue the god of money more than Almighty God.

Jesus told us to seek first the Kingdom of Heaven, and the other things will be added to us.

****

Manie sold the farm to a fine group of people and remained in the USA for several years and then moved back to South Africa.

Annie was healed of Cancer, and she and Bertus have finally joined me in the USA in the fulltime work of the ministry.

Sienie and Barry also surrendered their lives to Jesus and went back to school and graduated as a minister. She is ministering in South Africa and the USA.

Our workers on the farm, transferred to another ostrich ranch where they are working still today.

The two hoodlums on the kopje disappeared from the scene and I have no idea what ever happened to them.

Rock, is still a fine accountant and are now living in Cape Town, South Africa.

Piet, the detective is still regarded as one of the finest in Johannesburg.

Bernie and Adrie are back into calm waters, carrying on with their normal lives.

Our beautiful little Mother passed on to be with the Lord and we miss her greatly.

The President of Botswana suffered great financial losses on his ranch and finally retired from politics....